# APHASIOLOGY

Volume 18 Number 2 February 2004



CONTENTS

# APHASIOLOGY

First published 2004 by Psychology Press

Published 2021 by Routledge
2 Park Square, Milton Park, Abingdon, Oxon OX14 4RN
605 Third Avenue, New York, NY 10017

*Routledge is an imprint of the Taylor & Francis Group, an informa business*



The print edition of this journal is typeset by DP Photosetting

ISSN 1464-5041.

ISBN 13: 978-1-84169-976-9 (pbk)

APHASIOLOGY, 2004, *18* (2), 75–76

# Editorial

## Ten years of PALPAring in aphasia

The PALPA—Psycholinguistic Assessment of Language Processing in Aphasia (Kay, Lesser, & Coltheart, 1992, 1996)—has become a widely used resource for clinicians and researchers since its emergence from early progress in the development of cognitive neuropsychology.

Cognitive neuropsychology brought together researchers in cognitive psychology and neuropsychology, a modular model of the representation of function in cognition, and the detailed investigation of individuals with cognitive impairments. Early work concentrated on reading and writing, in particular, and speaking and comprehending single words. Later, modular models were developed through work with people with impairments in perception, action, memory, and number processing. Examination of impairments in language was conducted with tests controlled for relevant psycholinguistic variables, like word frequency, familiarity, concreteness, grammatical class, word length, etc. Within aphasiology, cognitive neuropsychological research has had a significant impact on our understanding of language processing. In more recent years, cognitive neuropsychology, together with developments in sophisticated brain imaging and connectionist modelling, has emerged as *cognitive neuroscience*.

Speech and language therapists/pathologists and clinical researchers working in aphasia were quick to see the clinical potential of the general approach of cognitive neuropsychology, with its concentration on detailed assessment aimed at locating deficits in specific modules or routes between modules within an explicit model. Such fine-grained testing allowed therapists to design treatments targeting areas of deficit more clearly. And so it came to pass that a new verb, *to palpa*, evolved and could be heard in a number of derived forms around aphasia departments in hospitals, clinics, and universities. Pioneers emerged who were seen to boldly palpa where no one had palpared before and PALPA became quickly established as a valuable resource for clinician and researcher.

While many were enthusiastic about replacing conventional standardised testing of aphasia with PALPA kinds of tests and the treatment that the approach inspired (Byng, Kay, Edmundson, & Scott, 1990), others were less so (Goodglass, 1990; Kertesz, 1990), suggesting that "standardised" assessment and classification was essential to planning treatment. In more recent years, clinical research has recognised the important contribution of a variety of approaches and a range of assessments are utilised in clinical aphasiology (Katz et al., 2001; Roberts, Code, & McNeil, 2003).

The PALPA resource was published in 1992 (see Kay et al., 1996 and commentaries), and 10 years later a new edition is in preparation. It is timely, therefore, that *Aphasiology* should host this Special Issue which includes papers from workers who are involved with the current and the future editions of PALPA. Janice Kay and Dick Terry report on the


http://www.tandf.co.uk/journals/pp/02687038.html DOI:10.1080/02687030344000508

use of the tests that make up the PALPA in the research literature over the past 10 years, and in three related papers Lyndsey Nickels and Jenny Cole-Virtue report on a series of investigations on the utility of different component tests. Max Coltheart presents some questions for the future development of the PALPA in research and clinical work.

*Chris Code*
*Exeter University, UK*

## REFERENCES

Byng S., Kay, J., Edmundson, A., & Scott, C. (1990). Aphasia tests reconsidered. *Aphasiology*, *4*, 67–91.

Goodglass, H. (1990). Cognitive psychology and clinical aphasiology: Commentary. *Aphasiology*, *4*, 93–95.

Katz, R., Hallowell, B., Code, C., Armstrong, E. Roberts, P., Pound, C. et al. (2000). A multi-national comparison of aphasia management practices. *International Journal of Language & Communication Disorders*, *35*, 303–314.

Kay, J., Lesser, R., & Coltheart, M. (1992). *Psycholinguistic Assessments of Language Processing in Aphasia*. Hove, UK: Lawrence Erlbaum Associates Ltd.

Kay, J., Lesser, R., & Coltheart, M. (1996). Psycholinguistic assessments of language processing in aphasia: An introduction. *Aphasiology*, *10*, 159–215.

Kertesz, A. (1990). What should be the core of aphasia tests? (The authors promise but fail to deliver). *Aphasiology*, *4*, 97–101.

Roberts, P. M., Code, C., & McNeil, M. R. (2003). Describing participants in aphasia research: Part 1. Audit of current practice. *Aphasiology*, *17*, 911–932.

APHASIOLOGY, 2004, *18* (2), 77–102

# Spoken word to picture matching from PALPA: A critique and some new matched sets

Jennifer Cole-Virtue and Lyndsey Nickels

*Macquarie University, Sydney, Australia*

*Background*: PALPA (Psycholinguistic Assessments of Language Processing in Aphasia; Kay, Lesser, & Coltheart, 1992) is a widely used clinical and research tool. Subtest 47, Spoken word–picture matching, requires the individual with aphasia to listen to a spoken word and correctly choose from five distractor pictures (target, close semantic, distant semantic, visually related, and semantically unrelated). It contributes diagnostically to the clinical evaluation of semantic processing. The authors claim that, first, errors on this test indicate that a semantic comprehension problem is present, and second, that distractor choice reflects the semantic specificity of the problem. For accurate clinical assessment the validity of these claims must be evaluated.

*Aims*: This paper aims to evaluate the internal validity of PALPA spoken word–picture matching. It addresses two questions; first, is the relationship between the target and distractors what the authors claim it to be? Second, what is the relationship between the target and distractor stimuli in relation to a number of psycholinguistic variables? In addition it allows the clinician to examine the effects of individual variables on performance by including matched subsets of stimuli from this test (matched across five psycholinguistic variables: frequency, imageability, number of phonemes, semantic and visual similarity, word association).

*Methods and Procedures*: Target and distractor relationships were investigated (in terms of semantic and visual similarity and word category) and psycholinguistic variables (including word frequency, word association, imageability, number of phonemes, semantic and visual similarity).

*Outcomes and Results*: Analysis revealed a number of confounds within this test: close semantic distractors were not only more semantically similar but also more visually similar to their targets than distant semantic distractors; the semantic and visual (SV) close semantic distractors were more semantically similar to their targets than the non-SV close semantic distractors; targets and distractors did not bear a consistent categorical relationship to their targets, and there were significant intercorrelations between variables for these stimuli (e.g., frequency and length; semantic/visual similarity and length).

*Conclusions*: The authors' claim that this test assesses semantic comprehension is certainly still tenable. Individuals making errors on this test have a high probability of some semantic processing deficit. However, this study shows that the test fails to assess the *nature* of the semantic processing deficit, as error patterns are subject to the effect of confounding factors. In its current form clinicians should exercise caution when interpreting test findings and be

Address correspondence to: Jennifer Cole-Virtue or Lyndsey Nickels, Macquarie Centre for Cognitive Science (MACCS), Division of Linguistics and Psychology, Macquarie University, Sydney, NSW 2109, Australia. Email: jenny@maccs.mq.edu.au or lyndsey@maccs.mq.edu.au

Thanks to Max Coltheart for helpful comments in the interpretation of these data, and to Stacey Kuan for help in collecting the semantic and visual similarity ratings. Janice Kay made useful comments on an earlier draft. Lyndsey Nickels was funded by an Australian Research Council QEII fellowship during the preparation of this paper.



http://www.tandf.co.uk/journals/pp/02687038.html DOI:10.1080/02687030344000346

aware of its limitations. The development, here, of matched subsets of stimuli allows performance to be re-evaluated in terms of the influence of semantic and visual similarity, imageability, frequency, word length, and word association.

For the practising clinician there are limited cognitive neuropsychological resources for the assessment and treatment of individuals with aphasia. The most widely used assessment materials are published in PALPA (Psycholinguistic Assessments of Language Processing in Aphasia; Kay et al., 1992), which has been an innovative and long-awaited contribution to the clinicians' armoury. PALPA includes a variety of language tasks with assessment and interpretation of findings based on a cognitive neuropsychological approach to language breakdown. Individual tasks within the battery are "designed to help illuminate the workings of specific components of the language processing model" (Kay, Lesser, & Coltheart, 1996a, p. 175).

However, there has been relatively little evaluation of the PALPA tasks and the importance of standardisation for the tasks included in the PALPA has been debated in the literature (e.g., Basso, 1996; Ferguson & Armstrong, 1996; Kay et al., 1996a, 1996b). Kay et al. (1992) provide some, but limited, detail regarding normative data, descriptive statistics, and control of variables before each task. Nevertheless, 14 (23%) of the 60 tasks have no normative data or descriptive statistics. Wertz (1996) perceives the lack of standardisation as a problem for the PALPA and comments that this may result in interpretative errors. "Standardisation provides consistency, validity provides comfort, and reliability provides confidence. The PALPA lacks all three" (Wertz, 1996, p. 188).

Validity is important, in terms of assessment and treatment planning, because clinicians are reliant on task validity as it "indicates that the measure does what we think it does" (Wertz, 1996, p. 184). The authors admit a shortfall and comment, "we have not carried out psychometrically satisfactory measures of validity or reliability" (Kay et al., 1996a, p. 160). However, they also respond by suggesting that measures of validity may not be appropriate (Kay et al., 1996b), as validity for PALPA is a question of whether the tasks measure the skills that they claim to and not whether this has validity to external factors, (e.g., anatomical localisation). It is just this question of internal validity that this paper seeks to address for one of the PALPA subtests: Spoken word to picture matching (subtest 47).

Spoken word–picture matching is located in the semantic processing section of PALPA. The aim of this task is to begin to assess semantic comprehension and, in conjunction with other semantic tasks, to enable the clinician to determine if a semantic deficit exists. Clinically, it is one of the most frequently used subtests, perhaps because of the prevalence of semantic processing disorders in aphasia and also that the authors suggest that clinicians use it as a starting point for their assessment of aphasia (Kay et al., 1996a).

As noted above, this task is widely used in speech pathology and neuropsychology as a clinical and research tool to assess language processing skills in people with aphasia. Indeed, in a review of publications citing PALPA, Kay and Terry (2004, this issue) found that it was the most widely used of the PALPA tasks. In both clinical and research settings it is utilised specifically for "testing semantic ability" (Marshall, Pound, White-Thomson, & Pring, 1990, p. 174) and to determine if a participant with aphasia has "a problem in gaining access to semantic information" (Forde & Humphreys, 1995). It frequently makes a significant diagnostic contribution to the clinicians' quantitative and qualitative evaluation of single word spoken comprehension and is utilised to direct treatment. It is therefore essential to consider whether impaired performance on this task can be interpreted with the confidence that is suggested by its authors, and that the clinical assessment of semantic comprehension ability is accurate.

In order to address this issue, we will investigate the nature of the relationship between target and distractor stimuli in a number of different analyses. We will first focus on the question of whether the relationships are those that Kay et al. (1992) claim in terms of semantic and visual similarity, and superordinate category. Second, we investigate further possible confounds in other psycholinguistic variables that may affect interpretation of performance on this test. Finally, we present some subsets of stimuli from this test that are matched for pertinent psycholinguistic variables.

## DESIGN OF THE TARGET AND DISTRACTOR STIMULI

Bishop and Byng (1984) were the first to address the use of different types of semantic distractors in a spoken word–picture match task. Their LUVS Test (The Test for Lexical Understanding with Visual and Semantic Distractors) was designed to assess semantic comprehension ability. They claimed that it was critical to include both semantic and unrelated distractors, to give the subject the opportunity to make semantic errors. Hence, systematic manipulation of distractor type was argued to help define the nature of the comprehension deficit. The PALPA spoken word–picture matching subtest 47 is based on similar principles and was adapted from the original LUVS assessment.

When performing this spoken word–picture matching task, a participant is required to listen to a spoken word and then select the correct picture from a choice of the target and four distractor pictures. There are 40 target items and the distractor pictures for each target consist of "a close semantic distractor from the same superordinate category, a more distant semantic distractor, a visually similar distractor and an unrelated distractor" (Kay et al., 1992, subtest 47, p. 1). For example, for the target word "carrot" the distractor pictures are "cabbage" (close semantic), "lemon" (distant semantic), "saw" (visually related), and "chisel" (unrelated) (see Figure 1). The unrelated and visually related distractors are related to each other semantically but not to the target item. This control feature has been incorporated to prevent the individual responding on the basis of perceived semantic category.

Qualitative evaluation of an individual's performance involves examination of error type. Kay et al. (1992) state that the distractors have been selected to reflect different semantic relationships with their targets. They claim that the pattern of errors reflects the degree and type of semantic processing impairments: A majority of close semantic errors suggests a relatively high-level semantic impairment. Close semantic distractors are divided into two groups, those that are purely semantically related to their targets (CSDnon-SV, e.g., carrot–cabbage) and those that are semantically *and* visually related to target (CSDSV, e.g., dog–cat). A majority of visually similar semantic errors (CSDSV) is argued to indicate that there may be a perceptual component to the deficit. Perceptual problems are also indicated if the individual tends to choose visually related distractors. The choice of the distant semantic distractor is argued to suggest a more widespread semantic deficit. Lastly, the choice of the unrelated semantic distractor error suggests that there is considerable difficulty in accessing any semantic information regarding the target.

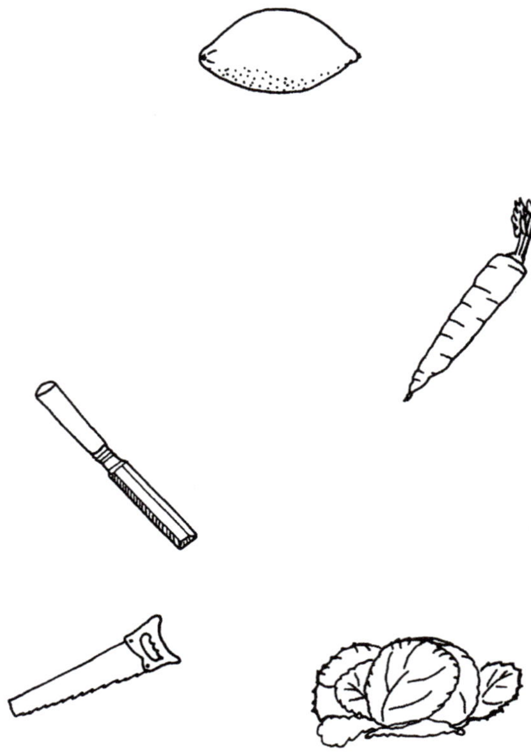

**Figure 1.** Item 1 from spoken word–picture matching, from PALPA (Kay et al., 1992; subtest 47).

## SEMANTIC AND VISUAL SIMILARITY OF TARGET AND DISTRACTORS

The nature of the distractors will be evaluated here in three ways.[1]

(1) Is there a difference in the degree of semantic similarity between targets and the close, distant, and unrelated distractors? Is it the case that there is the predicted gradient of semantic similarity across these items?
(2) Do close and distant semantic distractors differ purely in degree of semantic similarity to their targets, and not differ in visual similarity?
(3) Within the close semantic distractors, do the "semantic and visual" stimuli differ from the remaining (purely semantic) close distractors, only in the degree of visual similarity and not in terms of semantic similarity?

### Method

To evaluate the relationship between the distractors and the target items, we required a measure of the degree of semantic and visual similarity. Hence, we collected ratings of semantic similarity and visual similarity from 20 Australian non-aphasic participants,

[1] As semantic processing is our focus, here and throughout, we focus on the semantic and unrelated distractors, and do not consider the visual distractor in our discussions.

who were undergraduate psychology students and participated in the experiment as part of the fulfilment of their course requirements or for payment of $10. The participants were asked to judge how semantically similar or visually similar the close semantic distractor, distant semantic distractor, and unrelated distractor were to their corresponding target item. Participants made judgements of either semantic or visual similarity but not both. Participants were asked to use a rating scale of 1–7 to reflect whether words were highly unrelated (0), moderately related, or highly related (7) in meaning or appearance. For semantic similarity, it was emphasised that although some of the word pairs may also be visually similar, the focus for this judgement must be on meaning alone. As semantic processing is our focus, visual distractors were not included in these ratings. All pairs of stimuli were presented as written words in a pseudo-random order so that no target appeared within 10 items of a previous rating of that target.[2]

## Results

Ratings of semantic and visual similarity for each item and its close semantic, distant semantic, and unrelated distractors can be found in Tables 1A & 1B.[3]

*Semantic similarity across distractor types.* Consistent with Kay et al.'s claims, there is a significant difference in semantic similarity across the three distractor types (Page's L test: $L = 426.00$, $z = -6.97$, $p = .000$). Furthermore, close semantically related distractors are rated as significantly more semantically similar to their targets than both the distant semantic distractors ($t = 8.803$, $df\,39$, $p = .000$), and the unrelated distractors ($t = 24.961$, $df\,39$, $p = .000$). In addition, the distant semantic distractors were rated as significantly more semantically related than the unrelated distractors ($t = 12.012$, $df\,39$, $p = .000$). This semantic similarity gradient (CSD > DSD > URD) is true for 39/40 (97.5%) items. This is not the case for item 35 "needle" where the unrelated distractor (tweezers) is rated as more semantically similar to the target than the distant semantic distractor (spinning-wheel). Ideally, all items should consistently show semantic similarity gradients that are in the same direction.

*Visual similarity across distractor types.* Contrary to the authors' claims that the distractors differ in only semantic similarity, visual similarity was also found to differ significantly across the three distractor types (Page's L test: $L = 420.50$, $z = -6.67$, $p = .000$). The close semantically related distractors are rated as significantly more visually

[2] For ease of administration we chose to use word pairs, rather than picture pairs. It is possible that this will have resulted in different ratings than if we had used picture pairs. This is likely to have resulted in greater disparities for ratings of visual similarity than of semantic similarity, and for ratings of the visual distractors (not discussed here), than for ratings of other stimuli. However, as it is words that are presented as stimuli to be matched to pictures, we feel it is open to argument which rating is the relevant one for this task (and indeed which may vary from participant to participant). In fact, without knowing how an individual performs the task, and the effects of impairment on this process, it is impossible to adjudicate.

[3] Note that it is likely that the item "vest" had a low semantic similarity rating with its target because of dialectal differences between Australian and British English: In Australian English a sleeveless undergarment is called a "singlet" while "vest" refers to a "waistcoat". This, of course, would not be a problem for test administration as "vest" is not presented as a word, but simply as a distractor picture. In our opinion, the targets in this test are equally appropriate for Australian participants as for British (although we have received complaints from control participants on this task regarding the item "hosepipe" and insisting that 'hose' would be more normal, but this we feel would be equally likely to occur with British participants!).

TABLE 1A

Mean control ratings of semantic and visual similarity for 'non-SV' target and close semantic distractor pairs

| *Item No.* | *Target* | *CSD* | *SV/non-SV* | *Semsim* | *Vissim* | *DSD* | *Semsim* | *Vissim* | *URD* | *Semsim* | *Vissim* |
|---|---|---|---|---|---|---|---|---|---|---|---|
| 1 | carrot | cabbage | non-SV | 4.75 | 2.46 | lemon | 2.92 | 1.46 | chisel | 1.00 | 3.09 |
| 3 | hosepipe | bucket | non-SV | 4.00 | 1.60 | well | 2.33 | 1.40 | frog | 1.08 | 1.20 |
| 4 | hat | coat | non-SV | 4.00 | 2.18 | sock | 2.92 | 1.73 | ironing-table | 1.17 | 1.27 |
| 6 | belt | braces | non-SV | 4.00 | 4.09 | shirt | 3.08 | 1.91 | clock | 1.08 | 1.18 |
| 10 | moon | star | non-SV | 5.83 | 4.46 | planet | 5.17 | 5.64 | anvil | 1.13 | 1.57 |
| 12 | key | lock | non-SV | 5.58 | 3.55 | knob | 3.17 | 2.36 | flower | 1.18 | 1.27 |
| 13 | button | zip | non-SV | 5.17 | 3.09 | bow | 3.33 | 2.00 | banknote | 1.08 | 1.46 |
| 15 | syringe | stethoscope | non-SV | 3.42 | 2.00 | tablet | 2.17 | 1.36 | hinge | 1.17 | 2.27 |
| 17 | cobweb | spider | non-SV | 5.50 | 2.73 | ladybird | 1.67 | 1.64 | wagon | 1.00 | 1.36 |
| 20 | stirrup | saddle | non-SV | 5.17 | 3.40 | bridle | 5.09 | 4.63 | jacket | 2.00 | 1.33 |
| 22 | sword | shield | non-SV | 4.92 | 2.00 | gun | 4.00 | 3.27 | chain | 1.92 | 3.00 |
| 23 | comb | brush | non-SV | 6.83 | 5.46 | mirror | 3.58 | 1.82 | ant | 1.00 | 1.46 |
| 24 | eye | ear | non-SV | 5.75 | 3.18 | hair | 4.08 | 1.64 | bat | 1.33 | 1.46 |
| 27 | underpants | vest | non-SV | 3.58 | 3.36 | tie | 3.17 | 2.46 | watering-can | 1.00 | 1.09 |
| 29 | paintbrush | palette | non-SV | 5.00 | 2.73 | easel | 5.46 | 3.25 | kettle | 1.42 | 1.00 |
| 32 | pram | baby | non-SV | 4.67 | 2.46 | teddy | 2.92 | 1.82 | towel | 1.08 | 1.55 |
| 34 | hammock | cot | non-SV | 4.75 | 4.50 | pillow | 3.25 | 2.30 | cherry | 1.33 | 1.10 |
| 35 | needle | thimble | non-SV | 5.20 | 3.20 | spinning-wheel | 2.75 | 1.91 | tweezers | 3.17 | 4.00 |
| 37 | bell | whistle | non-SV | 4.46 | 3.91 | trumpet | 3.50 | 2.18 | battery | 1.42 | 1.91 |
| 40 | stamp | envelope | non-SV | 5.83 | 3.09 | pen | 2.42 | 1.82 | paint | 1.83 | 1.55 |

CSD: close semantic distractor; SV: close semantic distractor semantically related to target; non-SV: close semantic distractor semantically related to target; Semsim: mean semantic similarity rating; Vissim: mean visual similarity rating; DSD: distant semantic distractor; URD: unrelated distractor.

## TABLE 1B

Mean control ratings of semantic and visual similarity for 'SV' target and close semantic distractor pairs

| *Item No.* | *Target* | *CSD* | *SV/non-SV* | *Semsim* | *Vissim* | *DSD* | *Semsim* | *Vissim* | *URD* | *Semsim* | *Vissim* |
|---|---|---|---|---|---|---|---|---|---|---|---|
| 2 | dog | cat | SV | 5.42 | 5.18 | kangaroo | 3.25 | 3.27 | butterfly | 2.83 | 1.46 |
| 5 | axe | hammer | SV | 4.75 | 4.73 | scissors | 3.58 | 4.00 | kite | 1.00 | 1.36 |
| 7 | canoe | yacht | SV | 5.83 | 5.09 | lifebelt | 3.79 | 1.90 | bottle | 1.17 | 1.90 |
| 8 | ladder | steps | SV | 5.33 | 5.27 | rope | 3.42 | 3.00 | satchel | 2.00 | 1.46 |
| 9 | television | radio | SV | 5.58 | 4.55 | record-player | 4.17 | 3.64 | frying-pan | 1.08 | 1.73 |
| 11 | apple | orange | SV | 6.17 | 5.73 | grapes | 4.58 | 3.18 | necklace | 1.08 | 1.09 |
| 14 | stool | table | SV | 4.67 | 3.09 | sofa | 5.17 | 4.18 | switch | 1.27 | 1.46 |
| 16 | crown | tiara | SV | 6.56 | 6.60 | gown | 1.92 | 2.18 | bread | 1.00 | 1.27 |
| 18 | candle | match | SV | 5.33 | 4.09 | lamp | 5.17 | 4.73 | glove | 1.17 | 1.18 |
| 19 | lobster | crab | SV | 6.25 | 5.46 | fish | 5.58 | 4.64 | nut | 1.83 | 1.18 |
| 21 | cow | horse | SV | 4.33 | 5.00 | chicken | 4.00 | 2.00 | bed | 1.00 | 1.36 |
| 25 | rake | hoe | SV | 5.8 | 5.33 | scarecrow | 1.92 | 2.00 | salt | 1.00 | 1.27 |
| 26 | wall | fence | SV | 4.92 | 5.18 | house | 4.42 | 3.09 | rocking chair | 1.08 | 1.55 |
| 28 | nail | screw | SV | 5.42 | 6.55 | pliers | 3.46 | 2.36 | letter | 1.17 | 1.27 |
| 30 | parachute | balloon | SV | 4.58 | 5.00 | planet | 1.00 | 1.91 | puddle | 1.00 | 1.55 |
| 31 | dart | spear | SV | 5.42 | 5.73 | bow | 3.50 | 2.55 | razor | 1.92 | 2.82 |
| 33 | pipe | cigar | SV | 5.42 | 5.00 | ashtray | 4.08 | 2.27 | rolling-pin | 2.42 | 3.00 |
| 36 | thumb | finger | SV | 6.5 | 5.64 | leg | 2.92 | 2.18 | cigarette | 1.08 | 2.64 |
| 38 | shoe | boot | SV | 7.00 | 6.55 | trousers | 3.08 | 2.18 | monkey | 1.08 | 1.09 |
| 39 | mug | cup | SV | 6.75 | 6.91 | spoon | 3.67 | 2.64 | harp | 1.25 | 1.46 |
| | | | total mean | 5.26 | 4.25 | total mean | 3.49 | 2.61 | total mean | 1.37 | 1.66 |
| | | | SV mean | 4.92 | 3.17 | SV mean | 3.63 | 2.90 | | | |
| | | | non-SV mean | 5.60 | 5.33 | non-SV mean | 3.35 | 2.33 | | | |

CSD: close semantic distractor; SV: close semantic distractor semantically related to target; non-SV: close semantic distractor semantically related to target; Semsim: mean semantic similarity rating; Vissim: mean visual similarity rating; DSD: distant semantic distractor; URD: unrelated distractor.

similar to their targets than both the distant semantic distractors ($t$ = 6.408, $df$ 39, $p$ = .000) and the unrelated distractors ($t$ = 9.749, $df$ 39, $p$ = .000). In addition, the distant semantic distractors were rated as significantly more visually similar to the targets than the unrelated distractors ($t$ = 4.478, $df$ 39, $p$ = .000).

If we are to be confident that this test is a measure of semantic processing alone, visual similarity to the target should be held constant across distractors (excluding the visual distractors). As this is clearly not the case, we suggest that the visual similarity differences across distractors represent a confound in this test.

However, within the close semantic distractors, half the items (the CSDSV items) are *designed* to be visually similar to their targets. Hence, for the close semantic distractors, it is only the non-SV items that should be considered in terms of visual similarity. Nevertheless, even within this subset the close semantic distractors are still significantly more visually similar to their targets than the distant ($t$ = 2.566, $p$ = .007) and unrelated ($t$ = 5.238, $p$ = .000) distractors. This finding confirms that the distinction between the close and distant distractors is not one of semantic similarity alone and that another confounding factor, visual similarity, could affect error patterns on these items.

*Visual and semantic similarity within close semantic distractors.* These analyses compared the close semantic distractors that are claimed to be both semantically and visually related to their targets (CSDSV) with those that are claimed to be purely semantically related (CSDnon-SV). The CSDSV items were indeed rated significantly higher for visual similarity than the CSDnon-SV distractor items ($t$ = 7.300, $df$ 38, $p$ = .000). However, the CSDSV items were also rated higher for *semantic* similarity than the CSDnon-SV items ($t$ = 2.668, $df$ 38, $p$ = .011). In other words the CSDSV distractors are not only more visually similar but also more semantically similar to their targets than CSDnon-SV distractors.

This finding does not support the authors' premise and has implications for the interpretation of error patterns: A preponderance of errors on CSDsv items does not unequivocally indicate that it is the visual/perceptual component that is responsible for this pattern. As the CSDSV items are also more semantically similar, it would be expected that these items would be more error-prone as the result of a semantic impairment alone. Hence, it is impossible to know whether it is the visual component or the semantic component that results in relatively more CSDSV than CSDnon-SV errors.

## SEMANTIC RELATIONSHIPS OF TARGETS AND CLOSE SEMANTIC DISTRACTORS

Kay et al. (1992) make specific claims about the nature of the semantic relationship between the targets and their close semantic distractors. One of these claims is that the target and close semantic distractor pairs share the same superordinate category. For all 40 targets we examine the validity of this claim and seek to define the nature of the semantic relationship between these target pairs.

### Method

Twelve participants judged the relationship between the target and the close semantic distractor. They were asked to classify the items as coordinates (that is, from the same semantic category, such as, knife–fork; desk–chair) or semantically associated (things that go together in the world but are not part of the same semantic category; such as, desk–school; flower–vase).

## Results and discussion

Of the 40 target and close semantic distractor word pairs, 31 were considered to reflect a coordinate relationship. However, nine target and distractor pairs (hosepipe–bucket, key–lock, syringe–stethoscope, cobweb–spider, candle–match, paintbrush–palette, pram–baby, needle–thimble, stamp–envelope) were consistently classified as semantically associated rather than belonging to the same superordinate category.[4]

Hence, it is not the case that all of the target and distractor pairs share the same semantic relationship. For valid conclusions to be drawn from the analysis of error patterns in this subtest, the semantic relationships between the targets and their distractors need to be constant within each distractor type.

# PSYCHOLINGUISTIC PROPERTIES OF STIMULI FROM PALPA SUBTEST 47

In this section we will first examine two variables in detail, word association and word frequency. This will be followed by a brief examination of intercorrelations between a wider set of variables.

## Association of targets and distractors

A word association task consists of the subject being asked to say or write the first word that comes to mind for each target word (Lesser, 1981). Word association is thought to be a measure of the lexical relationship between two words, where they may not be semantically linked but often are found to co-occur in the same linguistic context or phrase, e.g., antique vase (Coltheart, 1980). Associative relationships between words have been discussed within the priming literature (see Neely, 1991, for a review). Shelton and Martin (1992) argue that associative priming results from connections between lexical rather than meaning representations. Word association is an important variable to consider in the context of a word–picture matching task, because if it is, in fact, a lexical rather than a featural or semantic measure then it is a potential confounding variable in terms of the semantic claims made for this subtest. Hence, we seek here to establish the nature of the word associations between the targets and distractors in this subtest.

### *Method*

To obtain a measure of the degree of association between the 40 targets and their distractors in subtest 47, the Edinburgh Association Norms were used (EAN; CISD, 1996). The measure of association used is the percentage of participants who produced a particular response to a target. A high percentage response indicates a high degree of association. Of the 40 targets, 5 (12.5%) (hosepipe, lobster, paintbrush, stirrup, underpants) were not found in the EAN and therefore could not be included in the analyses.

[4] It is possible that for some of these pairs a category could be generated to encompass both items. For example, "medical equipment" (syringe–stethoscope), "garden equipment" (hosepipe–bucket). However, the fact that none of our participants classified these items as belonging to the same category indicates that the categorical relationship is not primary. It is possible that a different design (e.g., tell me the category of these pairs of items) may have resulted in more of these "less automatic" categorisations.

## Results and discussion

*1. Are the targets and semantic distractors associated?* The close semantic distractor was produced in response to 24 of the remaining 35 targets (60%). For three of these targets (cobweb, dog, pram) the close semantic distractor was produced by more than 50% of the participants. The distant semantic distractor was produced in response to two (5%) of the targets. For 3 of the 35 targets (ladder, moon, mug) both the close and

TABLE 2
Edinburgh Association Norms for target-close and target-distant semantic distractor pairs

| *Target* | *Close semantic distractor (CSD)* | *% producing CSD* | *Distant semantic distractor (DSD)* | *% producing DSD* |
|---|---|---|---|---|
| apple | orange | 13 | grapes | 0 |
| axe | hammer | 2 | scissors | 0 |
| bell | whistle | 0 | trumpet | 0 |
| belt | braces | 2 | shirt | 0 |
| button | zip | 0 | bow | 1 |
| candle | match | 1 | lamp | 0 |
| canoe | yacht | 1 | lifebelt | 0 |
| carrot | cabbage | 1 | lemon | 0 |
| cobweb | spider | 66 | ladybird | 0 |
| comb | brush | 16 | mirror | 0 |
| cow | horse | 3 | chicken | 0 |
| crown | tiara | 0 | gown | 0 |
| dart | spear | 0 | bow | 0 |
| dog | cat | 57 | kangaroo | 0 |
| eye | ear | 9 | hair | 0 |
| hammock | cot | 0 | pillow | 0 |
| hat | coat | 24 | sock | 0 |
| hosepipe | bucket | TNF | well | TNF |
| key | lock | 30 | knob | 0 |
| ladder | steps | 12 | rope | 3 |
| lobster | crab | TNF | fish | TNF |
| moon | star | 2 | planet | 1 |
| mug | cup | 16 | spoon | 1 |
| nail | screw | 1 | pliers | 0 |
| needle | thimble | 0 | spinning-wheel | 0 |
| paintbrush | palette | TNF | easel | TNF |
| parachute | balloon | 0 | plane | 3 |
| pipe | cigar | 1 | ashtray | 0 |
| pram | baby | 58 | teddy | 0 |
| rake | hoe | 16 | scarecrow | 0 |
| shoe | boot | 4 | trousers | 0 |
| stamp | envelope | 4 | pen | 0 |
| stirrup | saddle | TNF | bridle | TNF |
| stool | table | 5 | sofa | 0 |
| sword | shield | 7 | gun | 1 |
| syringe | stethoscope | 0 | tablet | 0 |
| television | radio | 14 | record-player | 0 |
| thumb | finger | 2 | leg | 0 |
| underpants | vest | TNF | tie | TNF |
| wall | fence | 4 | house | 0 |

0: Distractor not found; TNF: Target not found

distant semantic distractor were found among the subject responses. For the remaining six targets (bell, crown, dart, hammock, needle, and syringe) neither the close or distant semantic distractors were produced in response to the target. See Table 2 for Edinburgh Association Norms for target-close semantic and target-distant semantic distractor pairs.

In summary, 29 of the 35 targets (72.5%) in the database show an association between either their close and/or distant semantic distractor.

*2. Does the degree of association vary across the distractors?* Ideally, the degree of association between the targets and distractors of different types should be constant, otherwise this presents another confounding factor for this test. However, the percentage of subjects in the EAN who produced the close semantic distractor in response to its target was significantly different from the percentage that produced the distant distractor for the same target ($t = 5.535$, *df* 34, $p = .000$). Hence, the degree of association is not constant across the close and distant distractors and may influence distractor choice.

*3. What is the relationship between semantic similarity and association?* Items that are semantically related can also be highly associated; for example 49% of participants produced the word "dog" when given the stimulus "cat". If semantic similarity and association were measures of the same relationship then it might be expected that items that are highly associated from the association norms would also be rated highly for semantic similarity. However, for the 35 target items in this subtest where association measures were available, there was no significant correlation between word association ratings and semantic similarity ratings for the same targets. The correlation was, in fact, negligible ($r = .051$, $p = .773$). This suggests that measures of semantic similarity and word association are reflecting different aspects of the relationships between items. This is further supported by the fact that Cole-Virtue and Nickels (2004 this issue) found that there was a facilitatory effect on semantic processing for items that had an associative relationship, whereas for semantic similarity, accuracy increased as the semantic similarity rating between items decreased. The opposite directions of these effects are consistent with the idea that measures of association reflect lexical-level relationships and the similarity ratings reflect a more semantically based relationship.

## Frequency of targets and distractors

The matching of stimuli for frequency in a semantic task attempts to control for the effect of that variable on that task. According to the Logogen model (Morton, 1970), at a lexical level, the lower the frequency of the item the less likely it is to be accessed correctly, as it has a higher threshold than a high-frequency item. Not only is the frequency of the target important but also the frequency of its neighbours, in this instance the semantic distractors. A low-frequency target is more likely to have neighbours or semantically related distractors that are of a higher frequency. If the semantic system is underspecified, as in aphasia, then this may influence performance on such a task. Hence matching both the target and the distractor for frequency ensures that once activated in the lexicon the reason that a target or its semantic distractor is selected should not be related to its frequency value, but rather reflects the nature of semantic processing.

The role and therefore the need to match items in terms of word frequency in semantic processing tasks is a contentious one. Bishop and Byng (1984) in their test (LUVS), matched distractor stimuli in their spoken word–picture matching task for mean frequency and frequency range. Silveri, Giustolisi, Daniele, and Gainotti (1992) also matched their target and distractor items for word frequency in a spoken word–picture matching task and noted that this was not a variable that affected subject performance. In an investigation of word–picture matching in Alzheimer's disease, Silveri and Leggio (1996) matched target and distractors on frequency range but the performance of the individual with aphasia was not evaluated in terms of this variable.

Kay et al. (1992) do not specify whether targets and distractors in their spoken word–picture matching task are matched for frequency. Here we investigate the relationship between targets and close semantic distractors, first using correlation. We found that the log frequency of targets and the log frequency of the close semantic distractor (CSD) are significantly and positively correlated ($r$ = .51, $p$ = .001). In other words, as the log frequency of the target increases so does the log frequency of the CSD. When we compared the log frequencies of the targets and their corresponding CSD, a $t$-test confirmed that there was no significant difference between them, $t(39) = 0.20$, 2-tailed, $p$ = 0.84. Similarly, we compared the log frequencies of the targets with their distant semantic distractors ($t$ = 1.142, $df$ 39, $p$ = .26) and log frequencies of the close semantic with the distant semantic distractor ($t$ = 1.015, $df$ 39, $p$ = .31) and found that they were not significantly different. This would suggest that the targets, their close semantic distractors, and distant semantic distractors are matched for log frequency. This is not surprising, as we know that subtest 47 was based on the original LUVS test (Bishop & Byng, 1984) and they matched distractor stimuli for frequency. As a result of the matching, the distractor choice should not be influenced by frequency. However, it is possible that frequency may still affect performance, as the targets themselves consist of higher and lower frequency items.

## Intercorrelations between psycholinguistic variables in the stimuli of PALPA subtest 47

### *Method*

Several psycholinguistic variables were examined using correlation. These variables include: spoken word frequency (Celex database; Baayen, Piepenbrock, & Van Rijn, 1993), familiarity, number of syllables, and phonemes (MRC database; Coltheart, 1981). Imageability values for 27 of the target items were taken from the MRC database and a further 8 from a set of object name norms (Morrison, Chappell, & Ellis, 1997). The Morrison et al. set of imageability ratings were linearly transformed so that they could be used in conjunction with those from the MRC database. The same method was used as for the merging of ratings from different sets of data in the MRC database (MRC Psycholinguistic Database User Manual: Version 1; Coltheart, 1981). Semantic and visual similarity ratings for the target–distractor pairs were also used (see earlier). Association norms for 35 of the 40 targets and their distractor pairs were from the Edinburgh Association Norms (CISD, 1996). The number of phonological neighbours for 39/40 of the target items was obtained using a programme written by David Howard (personal communication) to calculate number of phonological neighbours from the Celex database (Baayen et al., 1993).

### *Results and discussion*

A number of variables showed significant correlations within this test (see Appendix A). As expected there are strong correlations between variables that measure similar attributes, such as number of syllables and number of phonemes ($r$ = .84, $p$ = .000), frequency, and familiarity ($r = .38, p = .040$). It would be expected that words with more syllables would contain more phonemes, and that higher-frequency words are more familiar. In addition, some correlations followed the pattern generally found in the English language. There were significant (negative) correlations between number of phonemes and number of neighbours ($r = -.64, p = .000$) and frequency ($r = -.32, p = .042$): Short words (those with fewer phonemes) have more phonological neighbours (that is, more phonemes in common with other words) and are generally of a higher frequency than long words.

However, other variables, namely number of phonemes, semantic similarity, and visual similarity, show a correlation where a relationship would not necessarily be expected. Both semantic and visual similarity are negatively correlated with number of phonemes (semantic similarity $r = -.358$, $p = .023$; visual similarity $r = -.321$, $p = .043$). That is, longer target words are less semantically and visually similar to their distractor words than the shorter target words. This could make the longer target words easier to process, as they are more semantically and visually distinct from their close distractors.

## Summary

From the analyses presented above, we have established that there are a number of factors that reduce our confidence in interpreting the results of the PALPA spoken word–picture matching subtest (and will also affect the written word–picture matching subtest, which uses the same stimuli). These factors primarily relate to confounds between variables such as, for example, between semantic and visual similarity, or between word length and semantic similarity. One method that is used to reduce confounds between variables is to develop matched sets of stimuli which control for all relevant variables except the one of interest. Hence if one wished to examine the effects of semantic similarity on performance, two lists of stimuli would be generated which differ in semantic similarity but are identical for all other variables, such as word length, frequency, visual similarity. However, this is no easy exercise, because of the natural intercorrelations between variables in a language (see Cutler, 1981, for a discussion). Below, we present a series of matched sets, which are as well controlled as the limited range of stimuli, and high intercorrelations, allow. Taken together, these sets help overcome some of the limitations of PALPA word–picture matching subtest 47 and extend the generalisations that can be drawn from its use.

## Matched sets

As noted above, within subtest 47 we have shown that there are a number of highly intercorrelated variables and the matched sets presented here (Appendices B–F) are designed to control for some of these variables. These will allow for the effects of one variable on performance to be evaluated with confidence. Thus, having tested a person with aphasia on PALPA spoken word–picture matching subtest 47 (or written word–picture matching subtest 48), accuracy on each subset can be calculated. For all of the matched subsets a difference in scores (accuracy or errors) of five or more between the two conditions in a matched subset indicates that the variable being examined does have a significant effect on the individuals' performance. For those clinicians who may not have readily available access to statistical software, significance tables for the matched sets (calculated using Fisher Exact tests) are included in Appendices G–I. Many of these matched sets can, and should, be used in conjunction with one another to determine the nature of the influences on performance. It is important to note, however, that while the presence of a significant difference in accuracy across subsets can be interpreted as evidence for the effects of a variable on performance, the absence of a significant effect does not necessarily imply that there is no such difference—it may be that with a more powerful test with greater numbers of stimuli an effect might emerge.

There are five matched sets, all consisting of subsets of stimuli from PALPA subtest 47:

(1) *Close Semantic Distractor (SV) and Close Semantic Distractor (non-SV) matched for semantic similarity* (Appendix B). This set of 28 items contrasts those close semantic distractors that are classified as semantically *and* visually related to their targets (14 items) with those that are purely semantically related to their target (14 items). While in the test as a whole the close semantic SV and non-SV stimuli differed in semantic similarity as well as in visual similarity, this set is matched for semantic similarity (as well as for frequency, imageability, number of phonemes, and word association). Hence, these subsets differ significantly only in their visual similarity and therefore allow the clinician to determine the effect that visual similarity has on performance.

(2) *High–Low Semantic and Visual Similarity* (Appendix C). This subset contrasts 30 targets that were rated as highly semantically similar (15 items) and lower in semantic similarity (15 items) to their close semantic distractor. They differ significantly in their semantic similarity and are matched for frequency, imageability, and word association. A difference in performance on these conditions allows the clinician to determine the effect of semantic similarity on performance. It has been impossible to match these sets for visual similarity. However, note that the difference in semantic similarity between the high and low conditions is greater than the difference in visual similarity. If the individual shows no effect of visual similarity on the CSDSV/CSDnon-SV set then any difference on this set can be attributed to the effect of semantic similarity.

(3) *High–Low Imageability* (Appendix D). This subset of 30 targets examines the effect of imageability on performance; these are divided into 15 targets rated as high imageability (range 597–637) and 15 as lower in imageability (494–596). Note that the imageability range is necessarily self-restricting, as targets are all picturable items and these tend to be higher in rated imageability. The sets are matched for frequency, semantic similarity, visual similarity, number of phonemes, and word association.

(4) *High–Low Frequency* (Appendix E). This subset includes 28 targets, 14 that are higher frequency and 14 that are lower frequency. A difference in scores between these two conditions allows the clinician to determine the effect of frequency on performance. The sets differ in their frequency values and are matched for semantic similarity, visual similarity, imageability, number of phonemes[5] and word association.

(5) *Number of Phonemes* (Appendix F). This subset consists of 24 target items divided into two sets contrasting target word length. A difference in scores between these two conditions allows the clinician to determine the effect of word length on performance. The sets differ significantly in their word length but are not significantly different in semantic similarity, visual similarity, frequency[6] and imageability.

---

[5] Note, however, that while there is no significant difference between the number of phonemes in each set, the low-frequency set do tend to be longer. Hence, if an individual shows a strong effect of length on comprehension this could confound performance on this subset.

[6] Note however, that while there is no significant difference between the frequency of each set, the short set do tend to be higher in frequency. Hence, if an individual shows a strong effect of frequency on comprehension this could confound interpretation of length effects on this subset.

## GENERAL DISCUSSION

This paper has evaluated spoken word–picture matching from PALPA (subtest 47). There were two main components to this evaluation. First, to evaluate whether the relationship between target and distractors was what Kay et al. (1992) claimed it to be. Second, to evaluate the psycholinguistic properties of the stimuli. We will discuss each of these in turn.

### What is the relationship between the target and distractor stimuli in PALPA word–picture matching? (And is the relationship what the authors claim it to be?)

Kay et al. (1992) make three claims about this task: first, that it assesses the semantic processing ability of aphasic participants; second, that the distractors have been selected to reflect differing relationships with the target, consisting of semantically close, distant, visual, and unrelated items; third, that distractor choice or error type will reflect the nature of the semantic processing deficit.

Whether the relationships between the target and distractors fulfil the criteria that the authors' claim has been evaluated using three different measures, semantic similarity, visual similarity, and word category.

#### *Semantic and visual similarity*

The basis of the target–distractor relationship is the manipulation of the degree of semantic similarity. However, the authors give no information on how this was achieved or how it was measured, if indeed it was. This study analysed the target–distractor relationships using semantic and visual similarity ratings collected from unimpaired participants. The results and implications of these findings are mixed; the majority challenge the authors' claims regarding the interpretations of error patterns on this test.

In support of this test, the expectation across distractors is that the degree of semantic similarity with the target decreases through close to distant to unrelated distractor items. This was found to be the case, in that the close semantic distractors are more semantically similar than the distant distractors, and the unrelated distractors are less semantically similar to the target than both the close and distant distractors. This supports the authors' premise that there is a gradation of semantic similarity across distractors.

However, other findings contradict the authors' claims. First, although the distractors show a gradation of their semantic similarity relationship, the close distractors are not only more semantically but *also* more visually similar than the distant distractors. This disputes Kay et al.'s claim that the only difference between the close and distant distractor items is the degree of semantic similarity.

Moreover, the close semantic distractors are divided into items that are considered to be semantically and visually related (SV) and those that are purely semantically related (non-SV) to their target. The authors state that errors on the "SV" items are suggestive of a visual or perceptual component to an individual's impairment. Hence, the "SV" distractors and the "non-SV" distractors should differ from each other only on their visual similarity. Analysis showed that, in fact, the "SV" and "non-SV" distractors differed significantly not only in visual similarity but also in semantic similarity. The implication is that if a subject made a number of errors on "SV" distractors, the reason for that error may not always be due just to the visual component of the target–distractor relationship.

These inconsistencies not only put claims regarding the test in dispute, but also mean that the reason for error cannot be distinguished: both a visual impairment and a semantic impairment could influence subject responses.

### *Word category*

Kay et al. (1992, subtest 47, p. 1) state that the target and close semantic distractor items are from the same superordinate category. For the majority of the targets this appears to hold true, but for 22% of targets the relationship was judged to be one of semantic association, either by function or context. For accurate conclusions to be drawn from an individual's performance it is imperative that the relationships between these items is held constant and the authors claims regarding this relationship can only be rejected.

## What are the psycholinguistic properties of the stimuli in PALPA word–picture matching?

### *Word association*

Word association ratings are considered to be a measure of the lexical relationship between words. So words can be associated when not necessarily semantically linked. If the semantic similarity and word association ratings were to reflect a similar process, then a significant statistical relationship would be expected between them. This was not found to be the case and means that these variables are, indeed, measuring different aspects of the target–distractor relationship. The majority of the targets were found to be associated with either the close or the distant semantic distractor. This suggests that these items do not differ in the degree of semantic similarity alone and the association between the words may influence distractor choice. If we accept that this is another variable to be considered in the target–distractor relationship, it would be hoped that the degree of association might be held constant across the distractors. Unfortunately, this was not found to be so, as the target/close distractors were significantly more closely associated than the target/distant distractors.

The implication from these findings is that word association is a confound within this test and needs to be considered in the interpretation of performance.

### *Frequency*

There was a positive correlation between the frequency of the targets and the close semantic distractors. This means that as the frequency of the target increases so does the frequency of the close distractor. Further analysis showed that the targets and close and distant distractors are, effectively, matched for frequency providing some control for this variable in distractor choice.

### *Further variables*

Analysis showed that there were many other significant intercorrelations between the variables examined in this study (see earlier). The majority of the correlations were expected and in the predicted directions (e.g., word frequency and word length), however, one unexpected correlation did emerge: longer target words were less semantically and visually similar to their close distractors than shorter target words. The implication is that the longer target words may be advantaged, as they are more semantically and visually distinct from their close distractors.

In sum, there are a number of variables in this test whose possible effects have not been adequately considered in the test design. Many of these may affect performance on this test, therefore making the interpretation of distractor choice and identification of the specific variable that is affecting performance impossible. To help clinicians and researchers overcome these limitations we have presented some subsets of the stimuli that better control for relevant variables such as semantic and visual similarity, imageability, frequency, word association, and word length.[7] Finally, it is important to note that while we have focused on the spoken form of the test (subtest 47) the majority of the findings are directly relevant to the written word–picture matching subtest (subtest 48).

## CONCLUSIONS

At the time of publication the PALPA was, and still is in many respects, unique in its contribution to clinical assessment. It has allowed significant progress to be made in the clinical delineation of aphasia, utilising the tools of cognitive neuropsychological enquiry. However, it is now time for its stimuli to be evaluated more closely. This is imperative not only for the clinician, in terms of confidence in and the validity of their assessment, but also for the responsibilities that we have professionally to our clients. This study has attempted to fulfil these aims in two ways—first by evaluating and describing a number of limitations in one subtest of the PALPA, and second, by providing matched sets so that clinicians can address these problems and be confident of the outcomes that this test provides. Lastly, we hope that this is just the beginning: the task of clinical evaluation of the tools that we use is an ongoing process, and the only way is forward.

## REFERENCES

Basso, A. (1996). PALPA: An appreciation and a few criticisms. *Aphasiology, 10*, 190–193.

Baayen, R. H., Piepenbrock, R., & Van Rijn. (1993). *The CELEX lexical database* [CD-ROM]. University of Pennsylvania, PA: Linguistic Data Consortium.

Bishop, D., & Byng, S. (1984). Assessing semantic comprehension: Methodological considerations and a new clinical test. *Cognitive Neuropsychology, 1*(3), 233–243.

Cole-Virtue, J., & Nickels, L. (2004). Why cabbage and not carrot? An investigation of factors affecting performance on spoken word to picture matching. *Aphasiology, 18*, 153–179.

Coltheart, M. (1980). The semantic error: Types and theories. In M. Coltheart, K. Patterson, & J. Marshall (Eds.), *Deep dyslexia*. London: Routledge & Kegan Paul.

Coltheart, M. (1981). The MRC psycholinguistic database. *Quarterly Journal of Experimental Psychology, 33*A, 497–505.

Coltheart, M., Patterson, K., & Marshall, J. C. (1980). *Deep dyslexia*. London: Routledge & Kegan Paul.

Computing and Information Systems Department (CISD) (1996). *Edinburgh Associative Thesaurus*. Didcot, UK: Rutherford Appleton Laboratory UK.

Cutler, A. (1981) Making up materials is a confounded nuisance, or will we be able to run any psycholinguistic experiments at all in 1990? *Cognition, 10*, 65–70.

[7] An alternative method would be to investigate whether these variables have effects on comprehension for an individual using different stimuli (with greater numbers of items and hence greater sensitivity). If with adequate testing, the variables that confound spoken word–picture matchingt subtest 47 are not found to affect performance, then they are of less concern in the interpretation of performance on this subtest.

Ferguson, F., & Armstrong, E. (1996). The PALPA: A valid investigation of language? *Aphasiology*, *10*(2), 193–197.

Forde, E., & Humphreys, G. W. (1995). Refractory semantics in global aphasia: On semantic organisation and the access–storage distinction in neuropsychology. *Memory*, *3*(3/4), 265–307.

Kay, J., Lesser, R., & Coltheart, M. (1992). PALPA: *Psycholinguistic Assessments of Language Processing in Aphasia*. Hove, UK: Lawrence Erlbaum Associates Ltd.

Kay, J., Lesser, R., & Coltheart, M. (1996a). Psycholinguistic assessments of language processing in aphasia (PALPA): An introduction. *Aphasiology*, *10*(2), 159–179.

Kay, J., Lesser, R., & Coltheart, M. (1996b). PALPA: The proof of the pudding is in the eating. *Aphasiology*, *10*(2), 202–215.

Lesser, R. (1981). *Linguistic investigations of aphasia*. London: Edward Arnold Publications.

Marshall, J., Pound, C., White-Thomson, M., & Pring, T. (1990). The use of picture/word matching tasks to assist word retrieval in aphasic patients. *Aphasiology*, *4*(2), 167–184.

Morrison, C. M., Chappell, T. D., & Ellis, A. W. (1997). Age of acquisition norms for a large set of object names and their relation to adult estimates and other variables. *Quarterly Journal of Experimental Psychology*, *50*A (3), 528–559.

Morton, J. (1970). A functional model of memory. In D. A. Norman (Ed.), *Models of human memory*. New York: Academic Press.

Neely, J. H. (1991). Semantic priming effects in visual word recognition: A selective review of current findings and theories. In D. Besner & G. W. Humphreys (Eds.), *Basic processes in reading: Visual word recognition*. Hillsdale, NJ: Lawrence Erlbaum Associates, Inc.

Shelton, J. R., & Martin, R. C. (1992). How semantic is automatic semantic priming? *Journal of Experimental Psychology: Learning, Memory and Cognition*, *18*(6), 1191–1210.

Silveri, M. C., Giustolisi, L., Daniele, A., & Gainotti, G. (1992). Can residual lexical knowledge concern word form rather than word meaning? *Brain and Language*, *43*, 597–612.

Silveri, M. C., & Leggio, M. G. (1996). Influence of disorders of visual perception in word-to-picture matching tasks in patients with Alzheimer's disease. *Brain and Language*, *54*, 326–334.

Wertz, R. T. (1996). The PALPA's proof is in the predicting. *Aphasiology*, *10*(2), 180–190.

# APPENDIX A

## Intercorrelations between variables for target items in PALPA subtest 47

| | | *LF* | *Fam* | *Imag* | *Phones* | *Syll* | *CSD Freq* | *Semsim* | *Vissim* | *AoA* | *Assoc* | *Neigh* |
|---|---|---|---|---|---|---|---|---|---|---|---|---|
| | Mean | 0.7 | 535 | 594.2 | 4.18 | 1.53 | 0.68 | 5.26 | 4.25 | 264.31 | 10.60 | 11.97 |
| | St Dev | 0.75 | 57.17 | 25.88 | 1.85 | 0.72 | 0.72 | 0.87 | 1.43 | 83.43 | 17.17 | 10.20 |
| | Range Min | −0.3 | 379 | 494 | 1 | 1 | −0.3 | 3.42 | 1.6 | 167 | 0 | 0 |
| | Range Max | 2.45 | 611 | 637 | 9 | 4 | 2.42 | 7 | 6.91 | 394 | 66 | 0.03 |
| | N | 40 | 29 | 35 | 40 | 40 | 40 | 40 | 40 | 13 | 35 | 39 |
| LF | r | | 0.38 | 0.02 | −0.32 | −0.15 | 0.52 | 0.21 | 0.19 | −0.17 | 0.09 | 0.45 |
| | sig | | **0.040** | ns | **0.042** | ns | **0.001** | ns | ns | ns | ns | **0.004** |
| Fam | r | | | 0.04 | −0.54 | −0.30 | − 0.21 | 0.17 | 0.32 | −0.89 | −0.47 | 0.21 |
| | sig | | | ns | **0.003** | ns | ns | ns | ns | **0.000** | **0.014** | ns |
| Imag | r | | | | −0.01 | 0.19 | 0.12 | 0.20 | 0.09 | −0.33 | 0.04 | −0.09 |
| | sig | | | | ns | ns | ns | ns | ns | ns | ns | ns |
| Phon | r | | | | | 0.84 | −0.19 | −0.36 | −0.32 | 0.24 | 0.10 | −0.64 |
| | sig | | | | | **0.000** | ns | **0.023** | **0.043** | ns | ns | **0.000** |
| Syll | r | | | | | | −0.10 | −0.24 | −0.31 | 0.01 | 0.03 | −0.60 |
| | sig | | | | | | ns | ns | ns | ns | ns | **0.000** |
| CSD Freq | r | | | | | | | 0.08 | 0.06 | −0.25 | 0.20 | 0.20 |
| | sig | | | | | | | ns | ns | ns | ns | ns |
| Semsim | r | | | | | | | | 0.66 | −0.40 | 0.04 | 0.15 |
| | sig | | | | | | | | **0.000** | ns | ns | ns |
| Vissim | r | | | | | | | | | −0.16 | −0.25 | 0.23 |
| | sig | | | | | | | | | ns | ns | ns |
| AoA | r | | | | | | | | | | 0.48 | 0.28 |
| | sig | | | | | | | | | | ns | ns |

LF: log frequency; Fam: familiarity; Imag: imageability; Phones: number of phonemes; Syll: number of syllables; CSD Freq: log frequency of the close semantic distractor; Semsim: semantic similarity rating between target and close semantic distractor; Vissim: visual similarity rating between target and close semantic distractor; AoA: rated word age of acquisition; Assoc: word association; Neigh: number of phonological neighbours.; ns: non significant.

# APPENDIX B

Matched set for close semantic distractor-SV and close semantic distractor-non-SV

| No. of | SV set | | | | | | | | non-SV set | | | | | | | |
|---|---|---|---|---|---|---|---|---|---|---|---|---|---|---|---|---|
| *items* | *Target* | *CSD* | *Semsim* | *Freq* | *Imag* | *Vissim* | *Phones* | *Assoc* | *Target* | *CSD* | *Semsim* | *Freq* | *Imag* | *Vissim* | *Phones* | *Assoc* |
| 1 | dog | cat | 5.42 | 1.71 | 597 | 5.18 | 3 | 57.00 | carrot | cabbage | 4.75 | 0.00 | 602 | 2.46 | 5 | 1.00 |
| 2 | axe | hammer | 4.75 | 0.00 | 597 | 4.73 | 3 | 2.00 | hat | coat | 4.00 | 1.53 | 608 | 2.18 | 3 | 24.00 |
| 3 | canoe | yacht | 5.83 | −0.30 | 594 | 5.09 | 4 | 1.00 | belt | braces | 4.00 | 1.08 | 494 | 4.09 | 6 | 2.00 |
| 4 | ladder | steps | 5.33 | 1.08 | 612 | 5.27 | 4 | 12.00 | moon | star | 5.83 | 1.48 | 585 | 4.46 | 3 | 2.00 |
| 5 | television | radio | 5.58 | 2.45 | 599 | 4.55 | 9 | 14.00 | key | lock | 5.58 | 1.57 | 618 | 3.55 | 3 | 30.00 |
| 6 | apple | orange | 6.17 | 0.70 | 637 | 5.73 | 4 | 13.00 | button | zip | 5.17 | 1.00 | 580 | 3.09 | 3 | 0.00 |
| 7 | stool | table | 4.67 | 0.30 | 584 | 3.09 | 4 | 5.00 | sword | shield | 4.92 | 0.70 | 597 | 2.00 | 3 | 7.00 |
| 8 | candle | match | 5.33 | 0.70 | 577 | 4.09 | 6 | 1.00 | comb | brush | 6.83 | 0.60 | 592 | 5.46 | 3 | 16.00 |
| 9 | rake | hoe | 5.80 | 0.00 | 550 | 5.33 | 3 | 16.00 | eye | ear | 5.75 | 2.00 | 603 | 3.18 | 1 | 9.00 |
| 10 | wall | fence | 4.92 | 1.83 | 576 | 5.18 | 3 | 4.00 | paintbrush | palette | 5.00 | −0.30 | 601 | 2.73 | 8 | |
| 11 | nail | screw | 5.42 | 0.95 | 588 | 6.55 | 3 | 1.00 | pram | baby | 4.67 | 0.00 | 579 | 2.46 | 4 | 58.00 |
| 12 | parachute | balloon | 4.58 | 0.00 | 598 | 5.00 | 7 | 0.00 | hammock | cot | 4.75 | 0.00 | 562 | 4.50 | 3 | 0.00 |
| 13 | dart | spear | 5.42 | 0.00 | 636 | 5.73 | 3 | 0.00 | needle | thimble | 5.20 | 0.60 | 589 | 3.20 | 5 | 0.00 |
| 14 | pipe | cigar | 5.42 | 1.43 | 598 | 5.00 | 3 | 1.00 | bell | whistle | 4.46 | 1.69 | 610 | 3.91 | 5 | 0.00 |
| | mean | | 5.33 | 0.78 | 595.93 | 5.04 | 4.21 | 9.07 | mean | | 5.06 | 0.85 | 587.14 | 3.37 | 3.93 | 11.46 |
| | st dev | | 0.46 | 0.84 | 22.61 | 0.81 | 1.85 | 14.96 | st dev | | 0.76 | 0.74 | 30.54 | 1.01 | 1.73 | 17.14 |
| | | | | | | | | | *p*-value | | 0.27 | 0.79 | 0.39 | 0.00 | 0.68 | 0.70 |

CSD: close semantic distractor; Semsim: semantic similarity rating between target and close semantic distractor; Freq: log frequency; Imag: rated imageability; Vissim: visual similarity rating between target and close semantic distractor; Phones: number of phonemes; Assoc: word association; *p*-value: significance of a *t*-test comparing SV and non-SV sets.

# APPENDIX C

## Matched set for high–low semantic and visual similarity

| No of items | *High Sem/Vis sim set* | | | | | | *Low Sem/Vis sim set* | | | | | |
|---|---|---|---|---|---|---|---|---|---|---|---|---|
| | *Target* | *Semsim* | *Freq* | *Imag* | *Vissim* | *Assoc* | *Target* | *Semsim* | *Freq* | *Imag* | *Vissim* | *Assoc* |
| 1 | canoe | 5.83 | −0.30 | 594 | 5.09 | 1.00 | carrot | 4.75 | 0.00 | 602 | 2.46 | 1.00 |
| 2 | television | 5.58 | 2.45 | 599 | 4.55 | 14.00 | hosepipe | 4.00 | −0.30 | . | 1.60 | |
| 3 | moon | 5.83 | 1.48 | 585 | 4.46 | 2.00 | hat | 4.00 | 1.53 | 608 | 2.18 | 24.00 |
| 4 | apple | 6.17 | 0.70 | 637 | 5.73 | 13.00 | axe | 4.75 | 0.00 | 597 | 4.73 | 2.00 |
| 5 | key | 5.58 | 1.57 | 618 | 3.55 | 30.00 | belt | 4.00 | 1.08 | 494 | 4.09 | 2.00 |
| 6 | crown | 6.56 | 1.34 | 602 | 6.60 | 0.00 | stool | 4.67 | 0.30 | 584 | 3.09 | 5.00 |
| 7 | cobweb | 5.50 | 0.60 | . | 2.73 | 66.00 | syringe | 3.42 | −0.30 | 596 | 2.00 | 0.00 |
| 8 | lobster | 6.25 | −0.30 | 630 | 5.46 | | cow | 4.33 | 1.08 | 632 | 5.00 | 3.00 |
| 9 | comb | 6.83 | 0.60 | 592 | 5.46 | 16.00 | sword | 4.92 | 0.70 | 597 | 2.00 | 7.00 |
| 10 | eye | 5.75 | 2.00 | 603 | 3.18 | 9.00 | wall | 4.92 | 1.83 | 576 | 5.18 | 4.00 |
| 11 | rake | 5.80 | 0.00 | 550 | 5.33 | 16.00 | underpants | 3.58 | 0.00 | . | 3.36 | |
| 12 | thumb | 6.50 | 0.78 | 599 | 5.64 | 2.00 | parachute | 4.58 | 0.00 | 598 | 5.00 | 0.00 |
| 13 | shoe | 7.00 | 0.78 | 601 | 6.55 | 4.00 | pram | 4.67 | 0.00 | 579 | 2.46 | 58.00 |
| 14 | mug | 6.75 | 0.85 | 574 | 6.91 | 16.00 | hammock | 4.75 | 0.00 | 562 | 4.50 | 0.00 |
| 15 | stamp | 5.83 | 0.90 | | 3.09 | 4.00 | bell | 4.46 | 1.69 | 610 | 3.91 | 0.00 |
| | mean | 6.12 | 0.90 | 598.77 | 4.95 | 13.79 | mean | 4.39 | 0.51 | 587.31 | 3.44 | 8.15 |
| | st dev | 0.50 | 0.78 | 22.53 | 1.33 | 17.21 | st dev | 0.48 | 0.75 | 33.03 | 1.27 | 16.29 |
| | | | | | | | *p*-value | 0.000 | 0.173 | 0.312 | 0.003 | 0.392 |

Semsim: semantic similarity rating between target and close semantic distractor; Freq: log frequency; Imag: rated imageability; Vissim: visual similarity rating between target and close semantic distractor; Assoc: word association; *p*-value: significance of a paired-samples *t*-test across sets.

# APPENDIX D

Matched set for high-low imageability

| No. of items | High Imag set | | | | | | | Low Imag set | | | | | | |
|---|---|---|---|---|---|---|---|---|---|---|---|---|---|---|
| | *Target* | *Imag* | *Freq* | *Semsim* | *Vissim* | *Phones* | *Assoc* | *Target* | *Imag* | *Freq* | *Semsim* | *Vissim* | *Phones* | *Assoc* |
| 1 | carrot | 602 | 0.00 | 4.75 | 2.46 | 5 | 1 | belt | 494 | 1.08 | 4.00 | 4.09 | 4 | 2 |
| 2 | hat | 608 | 1.53 | 4.00 | 2.18 | 3 | 24 | canoe | 594 | −0.30 | 5.83 | 5.09 | 4 | 1 |
| 3 | ladder | 612 | 1.08 | 5.33 | 5.27 | 4 | 12 | moon | 585 | 1.48 | 5.83 | 4.46 | 3 | 2 |
| 4 | television | 599 | 2.45 | 5.58 | 4.55 | 9 | 14 | button | 580 | 1.00 | 5.17 | 3.09 | 5 | 0 |
| 5 | apple | 637 | 0.70 | 6.17 | 5.73 | 4 | 13 | stool | 584 | 0.30 | 4.67 | 3.09 | 4 | 5 |
| 6 | key | 618 | 1.57 | 5.58 | 3.55 | 2 | 30 | syringe | 596 | −0.30 | 3.42 | 2.00 | 6 | 0 |
| 7 | crown | 602 | 1.34 | 6.56 | 6.60 | 4 | 0 | candle | 577 | 0.70 | 5.33 | 4.09 | 6 | 1 |
| 8 | lobster | 630 | −0.30 | 6.25 | 5.46 | 6 | | comb | 592 | 0.60 | 6.83 | 5.46 | 3 | 16 |
| 9 | cow | 632 | 1.08 | 4.33 | 5.00 | 2 | 3 | rake | 550 | 0.00 | 5.80 | 5.33 | 3 | 16 |
| 10 | eye | 603 | 2.00 | 5.75 | 3.18 | 1 | 9 | wall | 576 | 1.83 | 4.92 | 5.18 | 3 | 4 |
| 11 | paintbrush | 601 | −0.30 | 5.00 | 2.73 | 8 | | nail | 588 | 0.95 | 5.42 | 6.55 | 3 | 1 |
| 12 | dart | 636 | 0.00 | 5.42 | 5.73 | 3 | 0 | pram | 579 | 0.00 | 4.67 | 2.46 | 4 | 58 |
| 13 | thumb | 599 | 0.78 | 6.50 | 5.64 | 3 | 2 | hammock | 562 | 0.00 | 4.75 | 4.50 | 5 | 0 |
| 14 | bell | 610 | 1.69 | 4.46 | 3.91 | 3 | 0 | needle | 589 | 0.60 | 5.20 | 3.20 | 5 | 0 |
| 15 | shoe | 601 | 0.78 | 7.00 | 6.55 | 2 | 4 | mug | 574 | 0.85 | 6.75 | 6.91 | 3 | 16 |
| | mean | 612.67 | 0.96 | 5.51 | 4.57 | 3.93 | 8.62 | mean | 574.67 | 0.59 | 5.24 | 4.37 | 4.07 | 8.13 |
| | st dev | 14.23 | 0.84 | 0.89 | 1.47 | 2.25 | 9.71 | st dev | 25.41 | 0.64 | 0.92 | 1.43 | 1.10 | 15.10 |
| | | | | | | | | *p*-value | 0.000 | 0.180 | 0.414 | 0.707 | 0.838 | 0.922 |

Imag: rated imageability; Freq: log frequency; Semsim: semantic similarity rating between target and close semantic distractor; Vissim: visual similarity rating between target and close semantic distractor; Phones: number of phonemes; Assoc: word association; *p*-value: significance of a paired-samples *t*-test across sets.

# APPENDIX E

## Matched set for frequency

| No. of items | *High Freq set* | | | | | | | | | *Low Freq set* | | | | | | | | |
|---|---|---|---|---|---|---|---|---|---|---|---|---|---|---|---|---|---|---|
| | *Target* | *CDSV* | *Freq* | *Celex* | *Semsim* | *Vissim* | *Imag* | *Phones* | *Assoc* | *Target* | *CD non-SV* | *Freq* | *Celex* | *Semsim* | *Vissim* | *Imag* | *Phones* | *Assoc* |
| 1 | dog | cat | 1.71 | 51.00 | 5.42 | 5.18 | 597 | 3 | 57 | carrot | cabbage | 0.00 | 1.00 | 4.75 | 2.46 | 602 | 5 | 1 |
| 2 | hat | coat | 1.53 | 34.00 | 4.00 | 2.18 | 608 | 3 | 24 | axe | hammer | 0.00 | 1.00 | 4.75 | 4.73 | 597 | 3 | 2 |
| 3 | belt | braces | 1.08 | 12.00 | 4.00 | 4.09 | 494 | 4 | 2 | canoe | yacht | −0.30 | 0.50 | 5.83 | 5.09 | 594 | 4 | 1 |
| 4 | ladder | steps | 1.08 | 12.00 | 5.33 | 5.27 | 612 | 4 | 12 | stool | table | 0.30 | 2.00 | 4.67 | 3.09 | 584 | 4 | 5 |
| 5 | television | radio | 2.45 | 285.00 | 5.58 | 4.55 | 599 | 9 | 14 | syringe | stethoscope | −0.30 | 0.50 | 3.42 | 2.00 | 596 | 6 | 0 |
| 6 | moon | star | 1.48 | 30.00 | 5.83 | 4.46 | 585 | 3 | 2 | lobster | crab | −0.30 | 0.50 | 6.25 | 5.46 | 630 | 6 | |
| 7 | key | lock | 1.57 | 37.00 | 5.58 | 3.55 | 618 | 2 | 30 | comb | brush | 0.60 | 4.00 | 6.83 | 5.46 | 592 | 3 | 16 |
| 8 | button | zip | 1.00 | 10.00 | 5.17 | 3.09 | 580 | 5 | 0 | rake | hoe | 0.00 | 1.00 | 5.80 | 5.33 | 550 | 3 | 16 |
| 9 | crown | tiara | 1.34 | 22.00 | 6.56 | 6.60 | 602 | 4 | 0 | paintbrush | palette | −0.30 | 0.50 | 5.00 | 2.73 | 601 | 8 | |
| 10 | cow | horse | 1.08 | 12.00 | 4.33 | 5.00 | 632 | 2 | 3 | parachute | balloon | 0.00 | 1.00 | 4.58 | 5.00 | 598 | 7 | 0 |
| 11 | wall | fence | 1.83 | 68.00 | 4.92 | 5.18 | 576 | 3 | 4 | dart | spear | 0.00 | 1.00 | 5.42 | 5.73 | 636 | 3 | 0 |
| 12 | nail | screw | 0.95 | 9.00 | 5.42 | 6.55 | 588 | 3 | 1 | pram | baby | 0.00 | 1.00 | 4.67 | 2.46 | 579 | 4 | 58 |
| 13 | pipe | cigar | 1.43 | 27.00 | 5.42 | 5.00 | 598 | 3 | 1 | hammock | cot | 0.00 | 1.00 | 4.75 | 4.50 | 562 | 5 | 0 |
| 14 | bell | whistle | 1.69 | 49.00 | 4.46 | 3.91 | 610 | 3 | 0 | needle | thimble | 0.60 | 4.00 | 5.20 | 3.20 | 589 | 5 | 0 |
| | | mean | 1.44 | 47.00 | 5.14 | 4.61 | 592.79 | 3.64 | 10.71 | | mean | 0.02 | 1.36 | 5.14 | 4.09 | 593.57 | 4.71 | 8.25 |
| | | st dev | 0.41 | 70.81 | 0.73 | 1.22 | 32.26 | 1.74 | 16.39 | | st dev | 0.30 | 1.18 | 0.85 | 1.35 | 22.38 | 1.59 | 16.76 |
| | | | | | | | | | | | *p*-value | 0.000 | 0.023 | 0.982 | 0.288 | 0.941 | 0.101 | 0.709 |

Freq: log frequency; Celex: spoken word frequency values from Celex database; Semsim: semantic similarity rating between target and close semantic distractor; Vissim: visual similarity rating between target and close semantic distractor; Imag: rated imageability; Phones: number of phonemes; Assoc: word association; *p*-value: significance of a paired-samples *t*-test across sets.

# APPENDIX F

## Matched set for number of phonemes

| No. of | Long set | | | | | | Short set | | | | | |
|---|---|---|---|---|---|---|---|---|---|---|---|---|
| *items* | *Target* | *Phones* | *Semsim* | *Freq* | *Imag* | *Vissim* | *Target* | *Phones* | *Semsim* | *Freq* | *Imag* | *Vissim* |
| 1 | needle | 5 | 5.20 | 0.60 | 589 | 3.20 | cow | 2 | 4.33 | 1.08 | 632 | 5.00 |
| 2 | button | 5 | 5.17 | 1.00 | 580 | 3.09 | key | 2 | 5.58 | 1.57 | 618 | 3.55 |
| 3 | candle | 6 | 5.33 | 0.70 | 577 | 4.09 | axe | 3 | 4.75 | 0.00 | 597 | 4.73 |
| 4 | syringe | 6 | 3.42 | −0.30 | 596 | 2.00 | bell | 3 | 4.46 | 1.69 | 610 | 3.91 |
| 5 | lobster | 6 | 6.25 | −0.30 | 630 | 5.46 | comb | 3 | 6.83 | 0.60 | 592 | 5.46 |
| 6 | canoe | 4 | 5.83 | −0.30 | 594 | 5.09 | dart | 3 | 5.42 | 0.00 | 636 | 5.73 |
| 7 | parachute | 7 | 4.58 | 0.00 | 598 | 5.00 | dog | 3 | 5.42 | 1.71 | 597 | 5.18 |
| 8 | paintbrush | 8 | 5.00 | −0.30 | 601 | 2.73 | hat | 3 | 4.00 | 1.53 | 608 | 2.18 |
| 9 | television | 9 | 5.58 | 2.45 | 599 | 4.55 | moon | 3 | 5.83 | 1.48 | 585 | 4.46 |
| 10 | belt | 4 | 4.00 | 1.08 | 494 | 4.09 | eye | 1 | 5.75 | 2.00 | 603 | 3.18 |
| 11 | carrot | 5 | 4.75 | 0.00 | 602 | 2.46 | pram | 4 | 4.67 | 0.00 | 579 | 2.46 |
| 12 | hammock | 5 | 4.75 | 0.00 | 562 | 4.50 | rake | 3 | 5.80 | 0.00 | 550 | 5.33 |
| | mean | 5.83 | 4.99 | 0.39 | 585.17 | 3.85 | mean | 2.75 | 5.24 | 0.97 | 600.58 | 4.26 |
| | st dev | 1.53 | 0.77 | 0.83 | 33.10 | 1.13 | st dev | 0.75 | 0.81 | 0.80 | 23.47 | 1.20 |
| | | | | | | | *p*-value | 0.000 | 0.451 | 0.092 | 0.202 | 0.399 |

Phones: number of phonemes; Semsim: semantic similarity rating between target and close semantic distractor; Freq: log frequency; Imag: rated imageability; Vissim: visual similarity rating between target and close semantic distractor; *p*-value: significance of a paired-samples *t*-test across sets.

# APPENDIX G

**Significance table for hi/low semantic/visual similarity set and imageability matched sets where $n = 15$**

| *Scores* | *4* | *5* | *6* | *7* | *8* | *9* | *10* | *11* | *12* | *13* | *14* | *15* |
|---|---|---|---|---|---|---|---|---|---|---|---|---|
| 0 | ns | .042 | .017 | .006 | .002 | .001 | .000 | .000 | .000 | .000 | .000 | .000 |
| 1 | | ns | ns | .035 | .014 | .005 | .002 | .001 | .000 | .000 | .000 | .000 |
| 2 | | | | ns | .050 | .021 | .008 | .003 | .001 | .000 | .000 | .000 |
| 3 | | | | | ns | ns | .025 | .009 | .003 | .001 | .000 | .000 |
| 4 | | | | | | | ns | .027 | .009 | .003 | .001 | .000 |
| 5 | | | | | | | | ns | .025 | .008 | .002 | .000 |
| 6 | | | | | | | | | ns | .021 | .005 | .001 |
| 7 | | | | | | | | | | .050 | .014 | .002 |
| 8 | | | | | | | | | | ns | .035 | .006 |
| 9 | | | | | | | | | | | ns | .017 |
| 10 | | | | | | | | | | | | .042 |
| 11 | | | | | | | | | | | | ns |

Any combination of scores that does not appear on the table is nonsignificant (e.g., 0 & 2; 12 & 14).

## APPENDIX H

Significance table for CSDSV/CSDnon-SV and frequency matched sets where $n = 14$

| *Scores* | *4* | *5* | *6* | *7* | *8* | *9* | *10* | *11* | *12* | *13* | *14* |
|---|---|---|---|---|---|---|---|---|---|---|---|
| 0 | ns | .041 | .016 | .006 | .002 | .001 | .000 | .000 | .000 | .000 | .000 |
| 1 | | ns | ns | .033 | .013 | .004 | .001 | .000 | .000 | .000 | .000 |
| 2 | | ns | ns | ns | .046 | .018 | .006 | .002 | .000 | .000 | .000 |
| 3 | | | | ns | ns | ns | .021 | .007 | .002 | .000 | .000 |
| 4 | | | | | | ns | ns | .021 | .006 | .001 | .000 |
| 5 | | | | | | | | ns | .018 | .004 | .001 |
| 6 | | | | | | | | | .046 | .013 | .002 |
| 7 | | | | | | | | | ns | .033 | .006 |
| 8 | | | | | | | | | | ns | .016 |
| 9 | | | | | | | | | | | .041 |
| 10 | | | | | | | | | | | ns |

## APPENDIX I

Significance table for number of phonemes matched set where $n = 12$

| *Scores* | *4* | *5* | *6* | *7* | *8* | *9* | *10* | *11* | *12* |
|---|---|---|---|---|---|---|---|---|---|
| 0 | ns | .035 | .012 | .004 | .001 | .000 | .000 | .000 | .000 |
| 1 | | ns | ns | .024 | .008 | .002 | .000 | .000 | .000 |
| 2 | | | | ns | .030 | .009 | .002 | .000 | .000 |
| 3 | | | | | ns | .030 | .008 | .001 | .000 |
| 4 | | | | | | ns | .024 | .004 | .001 |
| 5 | | | | | | | ns | .012 | .005 |
| 6 | | | | | | | | .035 | .014 |
| 7 | | | | | | | | ns | .037 |
| 8 | | | | | | | | | ns |

APHASIOLOGY, 2004, *18* (2), 103–126

# Reading tasks from PALPA: How do controls perform on visual lexical decision, homophony, rhyme, and synonym judgements?

Lyndsey Nickels and Jennifer Cole-Virtue

*Macquarie University, Sydney, Australia*

*Background*: PALPA (Psycholinguistic Assessments of Language Processing in Aphasia; Kay, Lesser, & Coltheart, 1992) is a resource widely used by both clinicians and researchers. However, several of the subtests lack data regarding the performance of proficient English language speakers on these tasks.

*Aims*: This paper investigates factors affecting the speed and accuracy of performance of young control participants on four assessments from PALPA: Visual lexical decision (subtest 25); synonym judgements (subtest 50); rhyme judgements (subtest 15); and homophone judgements (subtest 28).

*Methods and Procedures*: Data are presented regarding both speed and accuracy of performance on each of the four tasks, and statistical analysis of those factors that influence performance within each test is carried out, for the participants as a group and also for the individuals within the group.

*Outcomes and Results:* Visual lexical decision showed significant effects of frequency on response latency and accuracy, and of lexicality and imageability on response latency alone; synonym judgements showed significant effects of imageability on response latency; significant effects of word type were found on response latency for homophone judgements; for rhyme judgements there was a significant effect of rhyme for both accuracy and latency, and a significant interaction between rhyme and visual similarity.

*Conclusions*: For the clinician seeking to interpret the performance of the person with aphasia on the tasks we have described here, we have presented data that provide some indication of the speed and accuracy of performance of young controls on these tasks. It is clear that ceiling effects in accuracy mask effects of psycholinguistic variables on normal performance that become apparent when speed of response is considered. However, performance is far from at ceiling for all the tasks described—some participants perform close to chance on some conditions. Finally, these data highlight the fact that comparison of the pattern of performance of individual participants with that of a group of controls can be problematic given the variability of control patterns of performance.

Address correspondence to: Lyndsey Nickels, Macquarie Centre for Cognitive Science (MACCS), Macquarie University, Sydney, NSW 2109, Australia. Email: lyndsey@maccs.mq.edu.au

Lyndsey Nickels was supported by an Australian Research Council QEII fellowship during preparation of this paper. Thanks to Anna Woollams for programming the DMDX software, to Carl Windhorst for help running the experiments, and to Britta Biedermann for some of the analysis. Two reviewers provided helpful comments on an earlier draft and David Howard suggested the inclusion of effect sizes and their relationship to mean RT.



http://www.tandf.co.uk/journals/pp/02687038.html DOI:10.1080/02687030344000517

PALPA (Psycholinguistic Assessments of Language Processing in Aphasia; Kay, Lesser, & Coltheart, 1992) is a resource widely used by both clinicians and researchers. It has proved invaluable but is not without its weaknesses. One of these is the relative lack of data regarding how proficient English language users (so called "normal" speakers or "controls") perform on many of the tasks (Basso, 1996; Marshall, 1996; Wertz, 1996). The authors of PALPA suggest that one can assume that controls will perform at ceiling on the majority of the tasks—and indeed this *may* be true for tasks such as repetition and reading aloud. However, one is less confident regarding control performance on some of the more complex tasks (e.g., silent rhyme judgements) and those using abstract and low frequency vocabulary (e.g., synonym judgements). Hence, at least for these tasks, control data are required.

Moreover, there is an argument that tasks where most controls are performing at ceiling may not be optimal in terms of evaluating the performance of the person with aphasia (Kay, Lesser, & Coltheart, 1996). Best (2000) argues that performance with accuracy at ceiling may mask the fact that some subsets of stimuli in a task may be harder than others (e.g., visually similar rhyming pairs versus non visually similar rhyming pairs). This can make interpreting the performance of an individual with aphasia difficult. Furthermore, can we be confident that, by scoring at ceiling in terms of accuracy, the person with aphasia is performing as they would have premorbidly? Is the presence of, for example, worse performance on visually similar rhyming pairs significant or is it merely that these are also more difficult for controls (even if performance is accurate)? One way of avoiding ceiling effects on performance is to examine both accuracy and speed of response on a task. Measuring speed of response allows the relative difficulty of subsets within tasks to be assessed even when accuracy is at ceiling, and gives a more sensitive measure of "normal" performance. This is particularly valuable when assessing those individuals with more subtle impairments.

Thus, in this paper we investigate the performance of young control participants on four assessments from PALPA: Visual lexical decision (subtest 25); synonym judgements (subtest 50); rhyme judgements (subtest 15); and homophone judgements (subtest 28). The latter three assessments have no normative data provided, and visual lexical decision has accuracy data alone from 26 elderly participants (spouses of people with aphasia), and with some omissions regarding the overall performance (e.g., no overall measure of accuracy). Here we will present data regarding both speed and accuracy of performance on each of the four tasks, and statistical analysis regarding those factors influencing performance within each test. We will discuss the pattern shown by the groups of participants and also by individuals within the groups.

## METHOD

### Participants

The 21 participants in this study were all undergraduate students from Macquarie University who were speakers of Australian English. Of these, 17 were female and 4 were male, and the average age was 25.4 years (age range of 19–48 years). The students participated in the experiment as part of the fulfilment of their course requirements, or for payment of AUD$10.

## Materials

Four tasks were presented: visual lexical decision, synonym judgements, homophone judgements, and rhyme judgements. Stimuli were taken from PALPA (Kay et al., 1992; subtests 25,[1] 50, 28, and 15, respectively).

### *Visual Lexical Decision Task (subtest 25)*

The aim of this task is for the participant to decide whether a written letter string is a word. The lexical decision task contained 10 practice items and 120 test stimuli. The test items consisted of 60 nonwords and 60 words. The word stimuli were in four subsets of 15 items, each systematically varying imageability and frequency within the subsets (High imageability–High frequency, High imageability–Low frequency, Low imageability–High frequency, Low imageability–Low frequency). Words are matched across groups (pairwise) as far as possible for grammatical class, number of letters, syllables, and morphemes. Nonwords are derived from words by changing one or more letters, while preserving orthotactic and phonotactic legality. The manipulation of frequency and imageability across sets allows the effects of these variables on performance to be evaluated.

### *Synonym Judgement Task (subtest 50)*

In this task the participant has to judge whether two written words are similar in meaning—approximately synonymous. There were four practice items (car–automobile, tree–house, help–code, start–beginning) and 60 test word pairs. Of the stimulus items, 30 pairs comprised words of high imageability and 30 pairs words of low imageability. Within each set, 30 of the pairs are (approximately) synonymous requiring a yes response and 30 are unrelated in meaning requiring a no response. The high and low imageability sets are matched for word frequency. The difference in imageability between the sets allows the effect of this variable on performance to be evaluated.

### *Homophone Judgement Task (subtest 28)*

In this task, the participant has to judge whether a written word pair (e.g., prey–pray; bore–bow) or nonword pair (e.g., heem–heam; bick–blic) sound the same. The homophone judgement task has four practice items and 60 test word pairs. There are three subsets, each with 20 stimulus pairs; regular, exception, and nonword. Each subset comprises 10 homophonic and 10 non-homophonic word pairs. The non-homophonic pairs are matched for visual similarity to the homophonic pairs. This task allows the effect of stimulus type, lexicality, and word regularity on the generation of phonology from print to be evaluated.

### *Rhyme Judgement Task (subtest 15)*

The aim of this task is for the participant to judge if two written words rhyme. To complete this task correctly the participant has to derive phonology from the written word, segment off the rime, and compare the segmented stimuli. There were four practice

[1] The 120 stimuli from subtest 25 were presented together with the additional 40 stimuli that occur in subtest 5 (auditory lexical decision); we only report the data from the subset of 120 items that is consisted with the items in subtest 25 (visual lexical decision).

items and 60 test word pairs, in four subsets of 15 words each. Half of the stimulus pairs rhyme and half are non-rhyming pairs. In the rhyming pairs, half the words (spelling pattern rhyme: SPR) share the same orthographic body and a decision based on visual similarity will result in a correct response (e.g., town–gown). The other half (phonological rhyme: PR), comprise rhyming pairs that have different orthographic bodies and in these cases a correct judgement can only be made if the participant knows how the word sounds (e.g., bowl–mole). The non-rhyming pairs are also in two halves, half share the same orthographic bodies (spelling pattern control: SPC), and here the visual similarity may mislead (e.g., down–flown). The remaining half of the non-rhyming pairs (phonological control: PC) are visually dissimilar, and also share the same bodies as the rhyming pairs (e.g., hoe–chew, corresponding with shoe–screw in the rhyming pairs).

Hence these subsets allow the effect of visual similarity between the word pairs to be assessed in the rhyme and non-rhyme conditions. Here we have chosen to use more descriptive (and hopefully transparent) labels for these PALPA subsets, reflecting the rhyme and visual similarity manipulation: SPR = rhyme-vissim (rhyme, visually similar); PR = rhyme-novissim (rhyme, not visually similar); SPC = norhyme-vissim (no rhyme, visually similar); PC = norhyme-novissim (no rhyme, not visually similar).

## Apparatus

The experimental control programme DMDX (Forster & Forster, 2003) running on a Pentium III PC was used for presentation of the stimuli and the recording of responses for all four tasks.

## Procedure

Participants were tested individually and required to sit approximately 14 inches away from the computer monitor. All four tasks were presented in a single session with order of task presentation randomised across participants. However, due to individual testing constraints not all participants completed all four tasks (and equipment error resulted in some participant data being lost). Task instructions were given verbally by the tester and also visually on the computer screen. For example, the instructions for homophone judgement were as follows;

For this task, you will see pairs of words or nonwords,
your job is to decide if they sound the same,
as quickly as you can, without making errors,
DO NOT SAY THE WORDS ALOUD
If they sound the same, press +,
If they DO NOT sound the same, press −,
Press NEXT to start practice.

Instructions were essentially of the same format for all tasks with only the first two lines changing for each task; lexical decision "you will see a letter string, your job is to decide if the letter string is a real word or a nonword", rhyme judgments "you will see pairs of words, your job is to decide if the words rhyme", and for synonym judgements "decide if the words are similar in meaning".

Participants were instructed to make their decision as quickly as they could and press a + or − button on a response pad to indicate their decision. Participants had to respond by pressing the + button to indicate a yes response and the − button for a no response. Each task had a number of practice items and the tester provided feedback following completion of these items. The number of practice and stimulus items varied across tasks, as noted above. The participant was then instructed to continue to the test items. The inter-stimulus interval for all tasks was 1 second.

# RESULTS

## Visual Lexical Decision Task

### *Group analyses*

Reaction time and error data are presented in Table 1 (details of errors per item can be found in Appendices B and C). These data were analysed by-subjects and by-items using analysis of variance (ANOVA). In the by-subjects analysis the factors of lexicality (word, nonword), imageability (high imageability, low imageability), and frequency (high frequency, low frequency) were treated as repeated measures and used to evaluate mean reaction time and accuracy per participant. In the by-items analysis these same factors were treated as independent measures when used to evaluate mean reaction time and accuracy per item.

*Reaction time.* There was a significant effect on mean reaction time of lexicality by-subjects, $F(1, 20) = 61.75$, $p = .000$, and by-items, $F(1, 118) = 88.33$, $p = .000$.

TABLE 1
Latency and accuracy data for visual lexical decision, by-subjects

| | *Imageability* | | *Frequency* | | |
|---|---|---|---|---|---|
| *Mean reaction time* | *High Imageability* | *Low Imageability* | *High Frequency* | *Low Frequency* | *Mean* |
| Words (yes response) | 528.34 (60.31) | 553.74 (77.26) | 516.33 (60.49) | 567.40 (60.49) | 541.06 (67.07) |
| Nonwords (no response) | N/A | N/A | N/A | N/A | 638.24 (94.33) |
| Mean | | | | | 589.13 (76.60) |

| | *Imageability* | | *Frequency* | | |
|---|---|---|---|---|---|
| *Mean accuracy (SD)* | *High Imageability (n = 30)* | *Low Imageability (n = 30)* | *High Frequency (n = 30)* | *Low Frequency (n = 30)* | *Total (n = 60)* |
| Words (yes response) | 29.14 (0.91) | 28.71 (1.52) | 29.67 (0.58) | 28.19 (1.69) | 57.86 (1.74) |
| Nonwords (no response) | N/A | N/A | N/A | N/A | 57.38 (2.75) |
| Total (*n* = 120) | | | | | 115.24 (4.21) |

Note that the same 60 stimuli comprise the High and Low Imageability sets as the High and Low Frequency sets (i.e., there are four subsets, High Imageability, High Frequency; High Imageability Low Frequency; Low Imageability, High Frequency; Low Imageability Low Frequency).

Participants were faster to respond to words (requiring a yes response) than nonwords (requiring a no response). There was no significant effect of lexicality on mean error either by-subjects, $F(1, 20) = 1.38$, $p = .255$, or by-items, $F(1, 118) = 0.76$, $p = .386$.

Within the yes responses (words) there was a significant effect on mean reaction time of imageability and frequency both by-subjects—imageability: $F(1, 20) = 11.52$, $p = .003$; frequency: $F(1, 20) = 23.86$, $p = .000$—and by-items—imageability: $F(1, 56) = 4.73$, $p = .034$; frequency: $F(1, 56) = 16.15$, $p = .000$. However, there was no significant interaction between imageability and frequency either by-subjects, $F(1, 20) = 0.62$, $p = .0442$, or by-items, $F(1, 56) = 0.55$, $p = .461$.

*Accuracy.* There was no significant effect on accuracy of imageability by-subjects, $F(1, 20) = 1.18$, $p = .289$, or by-items, $F(1, 56) = 1.40$, $p = .241$. Frequency had a significant effect on accuracy both by-subjects, $F(1, 20) = 13.61$, $p = .001$, and by-items, $F(1, 56) = 16.65$, $p = .000$. There was no significant interaction between imageability and frequency on accuracy by-subjects, $F(1, 20) = 2.25$, $p = .149$, or by-items, $F(1, 56) = 2.10$, $p = .153$.

### *Individual analyses*

*Reaction time.* All but two of the participants (19/21, 90%) showed faster reaction times with high frequency than low frequency stimuli, and eight participants (38%) showed a significant advantage for high frequency stimuli. No participant showed a significant advantage for low frequency stimuli and those who showed numerically faster mean reaction times showed very small differences (6 ms and 14 ms).

More participants showed faster responses to high imageability stimuli than to low imageability stimuli (18/21, 86%) but few showed significant effects of imageability on performance (3/21, 14%). (Individual data can be found in Appendix D.)

*Accuracy.* Participant performance was generally too close to ceiling to make statistical analysis of errors viable for most individuals. However, while only one individual participant showed a significant effect of frequency on accuracy, every participant who showed a difference between high and low frequency stimuli showed worse performance on low frequency stimuli, with only one exception (and this participant only made two errors). In contrast, while once again one participant showed a significant effect of imageability on accuracy, there was much more variability, with five participants making more errors with low imageability than high imageability stimuli (as would be expected from the group analysis).

## Synonym Judgement Task

### *Group analyses*

One participant's data were excluded due to equipment failure.

Reaction time and error data are presented in Table 2 (for details of errors per item see Appendix E). These data were analysed by-subjects and by-items using analysis of variance (ANOVA). In the by-subjects analysis the factors of imageability (high, low) and synonymy (synonymous, non-synonymous) were treated as repeated measures and used to evaluate mean reaction time and accuracy per participant. In the by-items analysis the factors of imageability (high, low) and synonymy (synonymous, non-synonymous) were treated as independent measures and used to evaluate mean reaction time and accuracy per item.

TABLE 2
Latency and accuracy data synonym judgements, by-subjects

| *Mean reaction time (SD)* | *High Imageability items* | *Low Imageability items* | *Mean* |
|---|---|---|---|
| Synonymous pairs (yes responses) | 882.71 (172.28) | 1141.82 (310.90) | 1008.28 (231.54) |
| Non-synonymous pairs (no responses) | 980.02 (231.77) | 1129.06 (260.29) | 1053.22 (238.84) |
| Mean | 931.76 (195.80) | 1132.47 (267.97) | 1030.17 (226.45) |
| *Number correct (SD)* | *High Imageability* ($n$ = 15) | *Low Imageability* ($n$ = 15) | *Total correct* ($n$ = 30) |
| Synonymous pairs (yes responses) | 14.15 (0.75) | 13.40 (1.19) | 27.55 (1.43) |
| Non-synonymous pairs (no responses) | 14.75 (0.55) | 14.45 (1.15) | 29.20 (1.58) |
| Total ($n$ = 30) | 28.90 (0.85) | 27.85 (1.69) | 56.75 (2.15) |

*Reaction time.* There was a significant effect of imageability by-subjects, $F(1, 19) = 65.91$, $p = .000$, and by-items, $F(1, 56) = 38.25$, $p = .000$), on reaction time. Participants responded faster to high imageability than to low imageability items.

There was no effect of synonymy on reaction time by-subjects, $F(1, 19) = 2.40$, $p = .138$, or by-items, $F(1, 56) = 1.15$, $p = .287$. There was a significant interaction between synonymy and imageability by-subjects only, $F(1, 19) = 6.29$, $p = .021$; by-items: $F(1, 56) = 3.54$, $p = .065$. This interaction reflects the fact that for high imageability items responses to non-synonymous pairs were slower, and for low imageability items responses to synonymous pairs were slower.

*Accuracy.* There was a significant effect of imageability on accuracy by-subjects only, $F(1, 19) = 21.40$, $p = .000$; by-items: $F(1, 56) = 1.84$, $p = .180$, with higher accuracy on high imageability items. There was a significant effect of synonymy by-subjects, $F(1, 19) = 11.43$, $p = .003$, and by-items, $F(1, 56) = 4.54$, $p = .037$, with responses to non-synonymous pairs being more accurate. There was no interaction between imageability and synonymy by-subjects or items.

### *Individual analyses*

*Reaction time.* Every individual participant within the group was faster to respond to high imageability than low imageability stimuli, and this was significant for the majority of the participants (70%; see Appendix F). The mean effect size (Low imageability RT minus High Imageability RT) was 200.7 ms with 95% confidence limits from 152.7 ms to 248.7 ms.

*Accuracy.* As error rates were low, statistical analysis was not performed. Only four individuals (20%) showed worse performance on low imageability stimuli and in all cases the difference was only one item.

## Homophone Judgement Task

### *Group analyses*

Reaction time and accuracy data are presented in Table 3 (for details of errors per item see Appendix G). These data were analysed by-subjects and by-items using analysis of variance (ANOVA). Word type was further examined using related *t*-tests for by-subjects and independent *t*-tests for by-items analysis. In the by-subjects analysis the factors of word type (regular, exception/irregular, and nonword) and homophony (homophonic, non-homophonic) were treated as repeated measures and used to evaluate mean reaction time and accuracy per participant. In the by-items analysis the factors of word type (regular, exception/irregular, and nonword) and homophony (homophonic, non-homophonic) were treated as independent measures and used to evaluate mean reaction time and accuracy per item.

*Reaction time.* There was a significant effect on mean reaction time of word type by-subjects, $F(2,40) = 8.28$, $p = .001$, and by-items, $F(2,54) = 22.70$, $p = .000$. There was also a significant effect of homophony on mean reaction time by-subjects, $F(1,20) = 27.58$, $p = .000$, and by-items, $F(1,54) = 12.31$, $p = .001$. Participants were faster to respond to items that required a yes response, i.e., homophonic word pairs, than non-homophonic pairs. There was a significant interaction between homophony and word type only by-subjects, $F(2,40) = 50.14$, $p = .000$; by-items, $F(2,54) = 1.88$, $p = .162$,

TABLE 3
Latency and accuracy data for homophone judgement, by-subjects

| *Mean reaction time (SD)* | *Regular words* | *Irregular words* | *Nonwords* | *Mean* |
|---|---|---|---|---|
| Homophonic pairs (yes responses) | 955.03[1] (205.60) | 1067.73[3] (213.32) | 1265.34[5] (280.96) | 1096.03 (213.85) |
| Non-homophonic pairs (no responses) | 1157.40[2] (214.31) | 1131.90[4] (203.71) | 1315.21[6] (237.71) | 1201.50 (197.48) |
| Mean | 1051.47 (189.28) | 1098.66 (189.04) | 1287.52 (247.10) | 1144.26 (312.09) |
| *Mean no. correct (SD)* | *Regular words* ($n$ = 10) | *Irregular words* ($n$ = 10) | *Nonwords* ($n$ = 10) | *Mean total correct* ($n$ = 30) |
| Homophonic pairs (yes responses) | 9.33[1] (0.48) | 9.24[3] (0.70) | 9.19[5] (1.03) | 27.76 (1.04) |
| Non-homophonic pairs (no responses) | 9.14[2] (1.20) | 9.24[4] (0.89) | 8.67[6] (1.20) | 27.05 (2.67) |
| All items ($n$ = 20) | 18.48 (0.93) | 18.48 (1.12) | 17.86 (1.68) | 54.81 (2.77) |

[1] R: Regular.
[2] RC: Regular Control.
[3] E: Exception.
[4] EC: Exception Control.
[5] NW: Nonword.
[6] NWC: Nonword Control.

reflecting the fact that regular words show a larger effect of homophony on reaction time than either irregular words or nonwords.

*Accuracy.* There was no significant effect on accuracy by-subjects or by-items of word type—by-subjects: $F(2, 40) = 0.75, p = .479$, by-items: $F(2, 54) = 0.53, p = .593$—or homophones—by-subjects: $F(1, 20) = 1.22, p = .283$, by-items: $F(1, 54) = 0.70, p = .406$. There was also no significant interaction either by-subjects, $F(2, 40) = 2.84, p = .070$, or by-items, $F(2, 54) = 0.29, p = .749$, on accuracy.

The effect of word type was further analysed using paired (by-subjects) and independent (by-items) *t*-tests (see Table 4). There were no significant differences between groups in accuracy, but in reaction time, regular and irregular word pairs were significantly faster than nonword pairs, both by-subjects and by-items. Regular pairs were significantly faster than irregular pairs by-subjects but not by-items.

### *Individual analyses*

*Reaction time.* A total of 71% of participants showed the effect of word type that was true of the group (regular word pairs faster than exception word pairs which are faster than nonword pairs; see Appendix H).

All participants showed faster reaction times to regular words than to nonwords and this was significant for 71% of participants. Most participants responded faster to exception words than nonwords (only one did not and this was a very small difference—12 ms), but this was only significant for nine participants (43%). A total of 76% of participants showed faster responses to regular words but these effects were only significant for two individuals (10%).

*Accuracy.* As the group showed no significant effects on accuracy, individual analyses were not attempted.

## Rhyme Judgement Task

### *Group analyses*

Only 17 participants performed this task. Reaction time and error data are presented in Table 5 (for accuracy for each item see Appendix I). These data were analysed by-subjects and by-items using analysis of variance (ANOVA). In the by-subjects analysis

TABLE 4
*t*-tests of latency and accuracy data for word types in homophone judgement, by-subjects and by-items

| | *By-subjects* | | | | *By-items* | | | |
|---|---|---|---|---|---|---|---|---|
| *Word type* | *Mean RT* | | *Accuracy* | | *Mean RT* | | *Accuracy* | |
| | *t* | *p* | *t* | *p* | *t* | *p* | *t* | *p* |
| Regular vs irregular | 2.349 | .029 | 1.520 | .144 | 1.108 | .275 | 0.000 | 1.000 |
| Regular vs nonwords | 10.986 | .000 | −0.780 | .444 | 5.348 | .000 | 0.882 | .384 |
| Irregular vs nonwords | 6.776 | .000 | −0.322 | .751 | 5.135 | .000 | 1.040 | .305 |

TABLE 5
Latency and accuracy data for rhyme judgement, by-subjects

| *Mean reaction time (SD)* | *Rhyme* | *Non-rhyme* | *Mean* |
|---|---|---|---|
| Visually similar | 984.15[1] (217.80) | 1321.85[3] (263.94) | 1121.24 (215.66) |
| Non-visually similar | 1069.87[2] (229.81) | 1206.45[4] (210.69) | 1136.84 (209.53) |
| Mean | 1025.53 (214.27) | 1257.11 (219.10) | 1129.47 (208.71) |
| *Mean accuracy (SD)* | *Rhyme* ($n$ = 15) | *Non-rhyme* ($n$ = 15) | *Total* ($n$ = 30) |
| Visually similar | 0.353[1] (0.493) | 3.47[3] (2.98) | 26.18 (3.23) |
| Non-visually similar | 1.18[2] (1.24) | 1.88[4] (1.78) | 26.94 (2.28) |
| Total ($n$ = 30) | 28.47 (1.28) | 24.65 (4.40) | 53.12 (5.10) |

[1] SPR: Spelling Pattern Rhyme.
[2] PR: Phonological Rhyme.
[3] SPC: Spelling Pattern Control.
[4] PC: Phonological Control.

the factors of rhyme (rhyme, non-rhyme) and visual similarity (visually similar, non-visually similar) were treated as repeated measures and used to evaluate mean reaction time and accuracy per participant. In the by-items analysis the factors of rhyme (rhyme, non-rhyme) and visual similarity (visually similar, non-visually similar) were treated as independent measures and used to evaluate mean reaction time and accuracy per item.

*Reaction time.* There was a significant effect on mean reaction time of rhyme by-subjects, $F(16, 1) = 46.29, p = .000$, and by-items, $F(1, 56) = 45.54, p = .000$. Participants were faster to judge rhyming pairs than non-rhyming pairs. There was no significant effect on mean reaction time of visual similarity either by-subjects, $F(16, 1) = 0.69$, $p = .418$, or by-items, $F(1, 56) = 0.01$, $p = .935$. There was a significant interaction between rhyme and visual similarity both by-subjects, $F(16, 1) = 11.29$, $p = .004$, and by-items, $F(1, 56) = 5.88$, $p = .019$.

*Accuracy.* There was a significant effect on accuracy of rhyme both by-subjects, $F(16, 1) = 15.50$, $p = .001$, and by-items, $F(1, 56) = 18.12$, $p = .000$. There was no significant effect of visual similarity on accuracy either by-subjects, $F(16, 1) = 1.92$, $p = .185$ or by-items, $F(1, 56) = 0.72$, $p = .398$. The interaction between rhyme and visual similarity for accuracy was significant by-subjects, $F(16, 1) = 13.39$, $p = .002$, and by-items, $F(1, 56) = 7.210$, $p = .010$.

The interactions between rhyme and visual similarity are illustrated in Figure 1. For both reaction time and error, they reflect the fact that for rhyming items error rate and response time are both smaller when the stimuli are visually similar; in contrast for non-

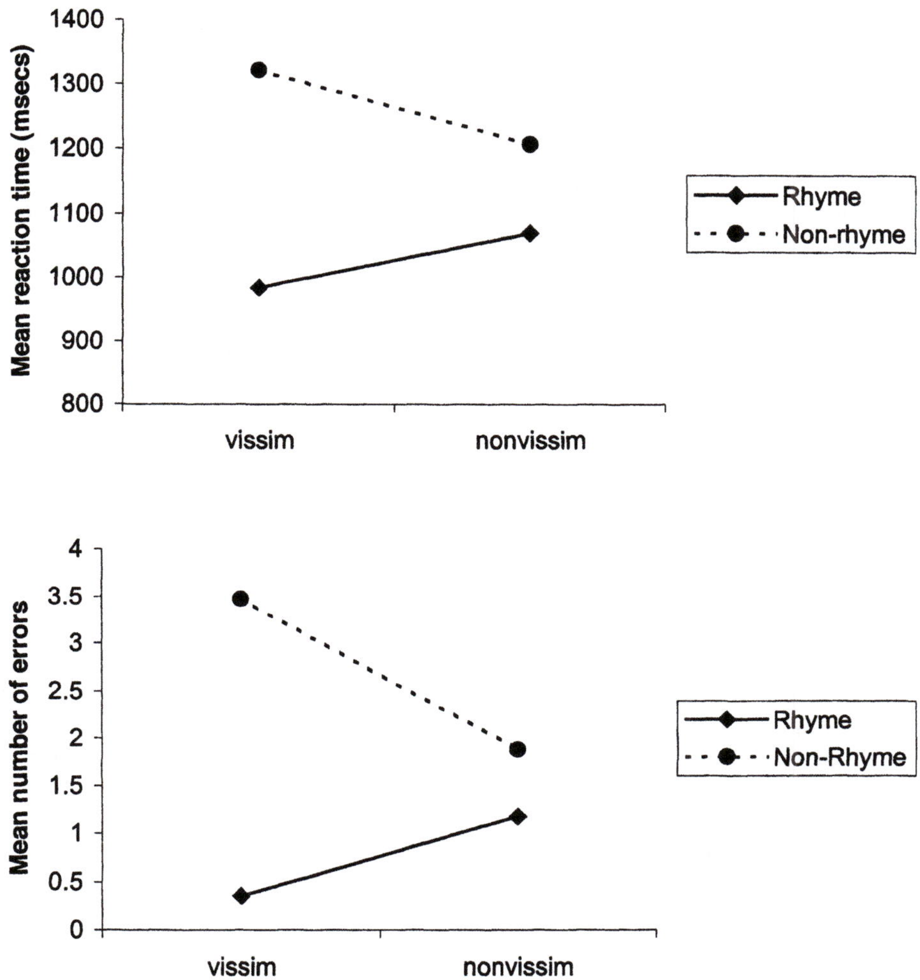


**Figure 1.** Interaction between effects of rhyme and visual similarity on reaction time and error rate in the rhyme judgement task.

rhyming items error rate and response time are smaller when the pairs are visually dissimilar.

Overall, the fastest and most accurate pairs were visually similar rhymes, then visually dissimilar rhymes, then visually dissimilar nonrhymes, with visually similar non-rhymes being the slowest and most error prone (*t*-test results presented in Appendix A).

### *Individual analyses*

*Reaction time.* Every participant showed numerically faster responses to rhymes compared to non-rhymes, and 10 of the participants (59%) showed significant effects of rhyme using ANOVA (see Appendix J). Again consistent with the group results no individual showed significant effects of visual similarity on reaction time. However, 5 individuals showed a significant interaction between rhyme and visual similarity, and 11 individuals showed the same pattern as the group with faster reaction times for visually similar rhymes and slower reaction times for visually similar non-rhymes.

*Accuracy.* Error rates were relatively high for some participants on this task. Indeed on some subsets some participants made over 50% errors.[2] All participants made relatively few errors on rhyming pairs. However, four participants made errors on a third or more of non-rhyming pairs overall.

Five individuals showed significant effects of rhyme on accuracy, and all but one participant showed better performance with rhyming than non-rhyming pairs. No participant showed a significant effect of visual similarity on accuracy and no clear pattern emerged (as predicted from the group data).

# DISCUSSION

We have investigated the performance of young control participants on four tasks from PALPA. A summary of overall mean accuracy and reaction time for each task is presented in Table 6, and those factors that significantly affected young control participant performance are summarised in Table 7. We will first summarise the results for each subtest before embarking on further discussion.

## Visual Lexical Decision

Participants were generally accurate on this task. There were no significant effects of lexicality or imageability on accuracy, although there was a significant effect of frequency, with the group performing less accurately with low frequency stimuli. In contrast, there were significant effects not only of frequency, but also of imageability and lexicality on speed of response (Nickels & Cole-Virtue, 2004). Individuals generally showed the same pattern as the group, and no participant showed a significant (or substantial) effect of frequency in the opposite direction to the group.

## Synonym Judgements

While generally accurate, only two participants produced no errors on this task. Effects of imageability were found for reaction times but for errors only by-subjects, and these were robust across individuals with no participant having slower reaction times to high imageability than low imageability stimuli.

## Homophone Judgements

There was more variability of accuracy on this task, with some participants scoring relatively poorly, particularly on nonword pairs. There were no significant effects on accuracy but word type (regular, exception, or nonword) significantly affected reaction time. The significantly faster response to regular words than to nonwords was robust across individuals.

## Rhyme Judgements

This task showed the greatest variability in accuracy and some subjects showed extremely poor performance on some subsets. There was a significant effect of rhyme for both accuracy and latency, which was moderately consistent across individuals. There was a

[2] While performance of 50% on individual subsets could be interpreted as being as chance, it is unwise to interpret the data in this way. Chance can only be interpreted over both "yes" and "no" responses, as error-free performance on one set and errorful performance on the other may simply reflect a bias to saying "yes" or "no".

TABLE 6

Summary of overall mean reaction time, and accuracy for four PALPA tasks, with values for a cut off of two standard deviations below the mean for each measure

| | | | Reaction Time | | | Number correct | | | Number of errors | | | Number of control participants |
|---|---|---|---|---|---|---|---|---|---|---|---|---|
| *Subtest No.* | | *n* | *Mean* | *SD* | *2 SD below* | *Mean* | *SD* | *2 SD below* | *Mean* | *SD* | *2 SD below* | |
| 25 | Visual Lexical Decision | 120 | 589.13 | 76.60 | 742.43 | 115.24 | 4.21 | 106.83 | 4.76 | 4.21 | 13.17 | 21 |
| 50 | Synonym Judgements | 60 | 1030.17 | 226.45 | 1483.08 | 56.75 | 2.15 | 52.45 | 3.25 | 2.15 | 7.55 | 20 |
| 28 | Homophone Judgements | 60 | 1144.26 | 312.09 | 1768.45 | 54.81 | 2.77 | 44.43 | 5.19 | 2.77 | 10.73 | 21 |
| 15 | Rhyme Judgements | 60 | 1129.47 | 208.71 | 1546.9 | 53.12 | 5.1 | 42.92 | 6.88 | 5.1 | 17.08 | 17 |

TABLE 7

Summary of those factors that significantly affected young control participant performance on four PALPA reading tasks

| | | Group effects significant for: | | % of individuals who show significant effects[1] | | % of individuals who show effects in the same direction as the group | | Effects reliable for all individual subjects | |
|---|---|---|---|---|---|---|---|---|---|
| *Task* | *Variable* | *Reaction time* | *Accuracy* | *RT* | *Accuracy* | *RT* | *Accuracy* | *RT* | *Accuracy* |
| Visual lexical decision | Frequency | ✓ | ✓ | 38% | 5% | 90% | 95% | | |
| | Imageability | ✓ | ✗ | 14% | 5% | 86% | 76% | | |
| | Lexicality | ✓ | ✗ | – | – | – | – | | |
| Synonym judgements | Imageability | ✓ | ✓* | 70% | – | 100% | 80% | ✓ | |
| | Synonymy | ✗ | ✓ | – | – | – | – | | |
| Homophone judgements | Word type | ✓ | ✗ | | – | 71% | – | | |
| | Reg vs Exception | ✓* | ✗ | 10% | – | 76% | – | | |
| | Reg vs Nonwords | ✓ | ✗ | 71% | – | 100% | – | ✓ | |
| | Exception vs Nonwords | ✓ | ✗ | 43% | – | 95% | – | | |
| | Homophony | ✓ | ✗ | – | – | – | – | | |
| Rhyme judgements | Rhyme | ✓ | ✓ | 53% | 29% | 100% | 94% | | |
| | Visual Similarity | ✗ | ✗ | 0% | 0% | – | – | | |
| | Rhyme* Visual Similarity | ✓ | ✓ | 24% | – | 65% | | | |

* By-subjects only.

As accuracy is often at ceiling, examination of effects on individuals was often not appropriate, see text for further discussion.

[1] All effects significant in the same direction as the group results.

significant interaction between visual similarity and rhyme, such that the group was faster and less error-prone for visually similar rhyming pairs, and slowest and most error-prone for visually similar non-rhyming pairs (although this pattern was not clear for individuals). Hence orthography has a marked effect on this phonological judgement.

## Comparisons between "normal" and "aphasic" performance

For the clinician seeking to interpret the performance of the person with aphasia on the tasks we have described here, we have presented data that provide some indication of the speed and accuracy of performance of young controls on these tasks. However, as Kay et al. (1996) note, these data cannot necessarily provide the answer to whether a particular individual with aphasia is performing on these assessments as they were premorbidly—this would require a group matched to that individual on, for example, age, educational history, occupation, and cultural background. Nevertheless, these data do help us on our way to deciding ''how many errors constitutes a deficit'' (Marshall, 1996).

However, there are also some cautionary messages to take away from our investigations, not least that controls can perform surprisingly poorly on what are intuitively straightforward tasks.

## Effects of variables on performance and inferring level of impairment

The discovery that a psycholinguistic variable affects the performance of the person with aphasia has frequently been interpreted to indicate an impairment of the stage of processing at which that variable is thought to operate. For example, an effect of frequency has been interpreted as evidence for a lexical level impairment, an effect of imageability for a semantic impairment. While it has been acknowledged that some of these variables also affect ''normal'' (speed of) processing there has been little discussion of the implications of this fact. If, as is the case here, ''normal'' subjects show effects of frequency on lexical decision (both for speed and accuracy) and imageability on synonym judgements, can we necessarily infer that the individual with aphasia who shows an effect of frequency is necessarily impaired in lexical access? Might it not be the case that this individual is showing the *same* effect of frequency that is the consequence of the normal system (but perhaps with a reduced overall level of accuracy)?

## Effects of variables on performance and individual variability

In the experimental investigation of language processing with so-called ''normals'', the standard methodology is to report group statistics, with little attention to the performance of individuals within the group. This is on the premise that the underlying language system is identical in humans (without language impairment and who are speakers of the same language) but that data are inherently noisy. Hence, by averaging across a group of individuals the ''noise'' is reduced and the ''true'' picture emerges. The difficulty with this approach is that in the clinical setting one is faced with a single individual, ''noise and all''! One approach that is used in research is to reduce the noise by multiple assessments or using very large samples of behaviour; clinically this approach is impractical. Hence, here we presented data from the individuals within the group in an attempt to ascertain how robust the effects were across individuals. For most effects the answer is "not very". The best that can be said is that no individual showed a significant result that was in the reverse direction to that of the group. Hence, little can be concluded from the lack of a significant effect (or absolute direction) of variables on performance, but if an individual shows a significant effect in the reverse direction to that of the group results reported here, that is more likely to be an indication of impairment.

## Effect sizes and their relationship to overall speed of processing

We have already discussed the extent to which effects were reliable across individual participants, and the problem of interpreting the behaviour of a particular individual with aphasia in relation to this (lack of) reliability. In Table 8 we present another means of summarising the data—in terms of mean effect sizes and the 95% confidence limits for that mean. Hence, for example, for synonym judgements low imageability stimuli were responded to on average slower than high imageability stimuli. The mean difference between the reaction times, the effect size, was 201 ms. The upper confidence limit is 249 ms and the lower 153 ms. In other words, based on this sample, 95% of the population will be between 153 and 249 ms slower to respond to low imageability stimuli in this synonym judgement task than to high imageability stimuli. It might, therefore, seem reasonable to conclude that an individual with aphasia who shows an effect size outside these limits is not performing "normally". Unfortunately this may be overly simplistic. Figure 2 shows the relationship between overall speed of response (overall mean RT) and size of the imageability effect (mean RT low imageability minus mean RT for high imageability). Each point in the scatterplot represents a single individual. There is a significant correlation between the two measures (see Table 8). In other words, the slower one is overall at performing synonym judgements the larger the difference between your speed of response to high and low imageability stimuli. This relationship is important, as individuals with aphasia are often slower to respond on such tasks than unimpaired controls (although this is not always the case). This slowing can be caused by a number of factors including the effects of age, brain damage, depression. Whatever the reason, clearly interpreting what is "normal" needs to take this factor into account, using the scatterplot as a guide. Table 8 shows that there is a significant relationship between effect size and overall response speed for several other of the tasks (visual lexical decision: frequency and imageability effects; homophone judgements: regular vs nonwords; exception vs nonwords; scatterplots shown in Appendix K). However, it is not the case that effect size correlated with overall speed of response for all tasks (homophone judgements: regular vs exception; rhyme judgements: rhyme and visual similarity effects).

## Comparison of an individual to a (small) group of controls

Thus far the message seems somewhat negative—control performance is variable and interpreting the performance of an individual person with aphasia is hence far from straightforward. However, there have been some statistical methods proposed that assist in this interpretation—providing us with estimates of an individual's "abnormality" and confidence limits on these estimates. Crawford and Howell (1998) present a technique for comparing an individual's score to that of a small group of controls (modified independent samples *t*-test rather than *z*-score as is more usual for normative data from a large sample). This technique would be appropriate for the tasks reported here, to establish whether an individual showed speed or accuracy of performance that is significantly

TABLE 8

Mean effect sizes (RT), 95% confidence intervals and correlation of effect size, and mean RT

| | | | | *95% confidence intevals* | | *Correlation with mean RT* | |
|---|---|---|---|---|---|---|---|
| *Task* | *Variable* | *Direction of calculation* | *Mean effect size (ms)* | *Upper* | *Lower* | *r* | *p =* |
| Visual lexical decision | Frequency | Low Freq – High Freq | 51.1 | 71.9 | 30.3 | .436 | .048 |
| | Imageability | Low Image – High Image | 25.4 | 40.7 | 10.1 | .489 | .024 |
| Synonym judgements | Imageability | Low Image – High Image | 200.7 | 248.7 | 152.7 | .668 | .001 |
| Homophone judgements | Reg vs Exception | Exception – regular | 47.5 | 87.1 | 7.9 | −.059 | ns |
| | Reg vs Nonwords | Nonwords – regular | 236.4 | 278.5 | 194.2 | .566 | .008 |
| | Exception vs Nonwords | Nonwords – exception | 188.9 | 243.5 | 134.2 | .480 | .028 |
| Rhyme judgements | Rhyme | Nonrhyme – rhyme | 231.6 | 295.2 | 168.0 | −.020 | ns |
| | Visual Similarity | Nonvissim – vissim | 15.6 | 50.3 | −19.1 | −.082 | ns |

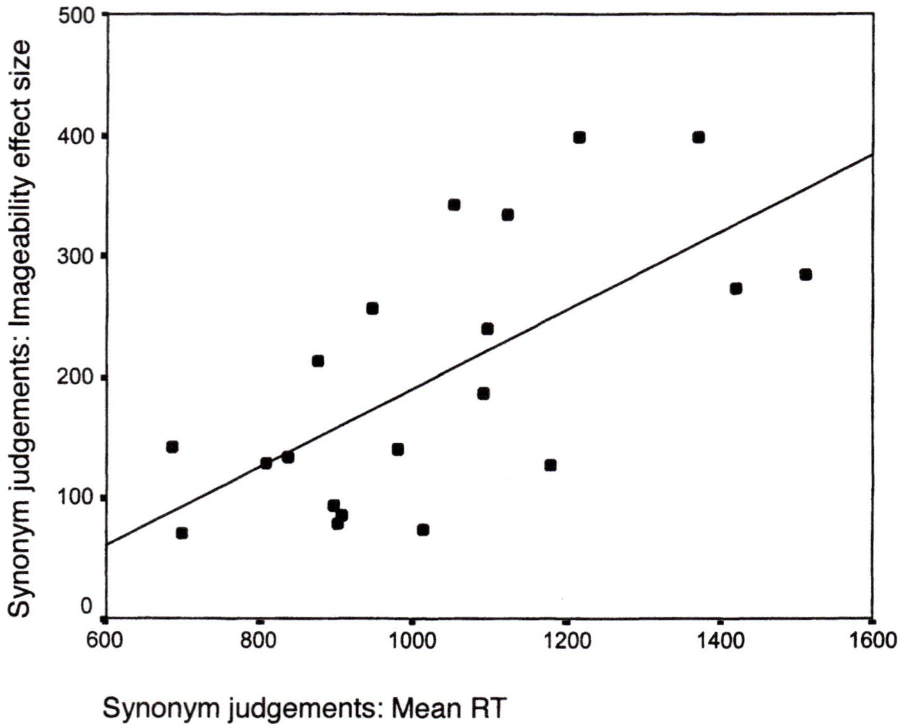


**Figure 2.** Scatterplot of the relationship between size of the imageability effect (reaction time difference) and overall mean reaction time for synonym judgements.

different from the control group. Crawford, Howell, and Garthwaite (1998) extend the analysis to allow comparison of the difference between performance on two tasks (using modified paired samples *t*-test). For the tasks presented here this analysis would be appropriate for establishing whether the difference between speed (or accuracy) of two conditions was within the norm. For example, comparing the difference between high and low frequency stimuli on lexical decision, or between high and low imageability stimuli in synonym judgements. Crawford and Garthwaite (2002) extend these methods further and incorporate an estimation of the confidence limits of the results.[3] This allows an estimation not only of what proportion of the normal population would score lower (or respond slower) on a task, but also what the upper confidence limits are on this estimation. These statistical tools help in the comparison of single cases to groups of control participants, although problems still remain by virtue of the variability in the normal population.

## SUMMARY

We have presented data from young Australian control participants performing four reading tasks from PALPA. The data from these young non-aphasic participants have confirmed the following for some of these tasks:

[3] Computer programs for performing these calculations can be obtained are made available by John Crawford and are downloadable from: http://www.abdn.ac.uk/~psy086/dept/abnolims.htm

- Ceiling effects in accuracy mask effects of psycholinguistic variables on normal performance that become apparent when speed of response is considered.
- The assumption of PALPA's creators that performance will be close to ceiling in accuracy is clearly erroneous for some of these tasks. Indeed, some participants perform remarkably poorly on some conditions.
- Comparison of details of the pattern of performance for individual participants with that of a group of controls can be problematic given the variability within the controls. However, for at least some tasks there are reliable patterns of performance across individual controls.

These data will provide essential further information for clinicians and researchers alike when interpreting performance on these four PALPA subtests, and reinforce the importance of evaluating performance in terms of both speed and accuracy.

## REFERENCES


Basso, A. (1996). PALPA: An appreciation and a few criticisms. *Aphasiology, 10*, 190–193.

Best, W. M. (2000). Category-specific semantic disorders. In W. Best, K. Bryan, & J. Maxim (Eds.), *Semantic processing in theory and practice*. London: Whurr.

Crawford, J. R., & Garthwaite, P. H. (2002). Investigation of the single case in neuropsychology: Confidence limits on the abnormality of test scores and test score differences. *Neuropsychologia, 40*, 1196–1208.

Crawford, J. R., & Howell, D. C. (1998). Regression equations in clinical neuropsychology: An evaluation of statistical methods for comparing predicted and observed scores. *Journal of Clinical and Experimental Neuropsychology, 20*, 755–762.

Crawford, J. R., Howell, D. C., & Garthwaite, P. H. (1998). Payne and Jones revisited: Estimating the abnormality of test score differences using a modified paired samples t-test. *Journal of Clinical and Experimental Neuropsychology, 20*, 898–905.

Forster, K. I., & Forster, J. C. (2003). DMDX: A Windows display program with millisecond accuracy. *Behavior Research Methods, Instruments & Computers, 35*, 116–124.

Kay, J., Lesser, R., & Coltheart, M. (1992). PALPA: *Psycholinguistic Assessments of Language Processing in Aphasia*. Hove, UK: Lawrence Erlbaum Associates Ltd.

Kay, J., Lesser, R., & Coltheart, M. (1996). PALPA: The proof of the pudding is in the eating. *Aphasiology, 10*, 202–215.

Marshall, J. (1996). The PALPA: A commentary and consideration of the clinical implications. *Aphasiology, 10*, 197–202.

Nickels, L. A., & Cole-Virtue, J. C. (2004). *Effects of imageability on lexical decision latency*. Manuscript in preparation.

Wertz, R. T. (1996). The PALPA's proof is in the predicting. *Aphasiology, 10*, 180–190.

# APPENDIX A

Comparisons of rhyme judgement subtests using *t*-tests

| | *no rhyme-nonvissim* | | *rhyme-vissim* | | *rhyme-nonvissim* | |
|---|---|---|---|---|---|---|
| | *t* | *p* | *t* | *p* | *t* | *p* |
| **By subject** | | | | | | |
| *Reaction time* | | | | | | |
| No rhyme-vissim | 2.957 | .009 | −6.314 | <.001 | −5.82 | <.001 |
| No rhyme-nonvissim | | | −6.439 | <.001 | −3.702 | .002 |
| Rhyme-vissim | | | | | −2.85 | .012 |
| *Error* | | | | | | |
| No rhyme-vissim | 3.128 | .006 | −4.585 | <.001 | −3.226 | .005 |
| No rhyme-nonvissim | | | −4.443 | <.001 | −1.484 | .157 |
| Rhyme-vissim | | | | | −2.46 | .026 |
| **By item** | | | | | | |
| *Reaction time* | | | | | | |
| No rhyme-vissim | 1.914 | .066 | 6.353 | <.001 | 5.484 | <.001 |
| No rhyme-nonvissim | | | 4.301 | <.001 | 3.125 | .004 |
| Rhyme-vissim | | | | | −1.585 | .124 |
| *Error* | | | | | | |
| No rhyme-vissim | 1.889 | .69 | 4.743 | <.001 | 3.276 | .004 |
| No rhyme-nonvissim | | | 2.719 | .015 | 1.153 | .259 |
| Rhyme-vissim | | | | | −2.606 | .015 |

# APPENDICES B–J

These appendices can be downloaded from:
http://www.maccs.mq.edu.au/~lyndsey/papers/N&C-V_2004_Appendices.xls

Appendix B: Visual lexical decision item accuracy data for word stimuli
Appendix C: Visual lexical decision accuracy data for nonword stimuli
Appendix D: Individual participant analyses for visual lexical decision
Appendix E: Synonym judgements item accuracy data
Appendix F: Individual participant analyses for synonym judgements
Appendix G: Homophone judgements item accuracy data
Appendix H: Individual participant analyses for homophone judgements
Appendix I: Rhyme judgements item accuracy data
Appendix J: Individual participant analyses for rhyme judgements

# APPENDIX K

## Scatterplots of the relationship between effect size and mean RT

(1) Lexical decision & frequency

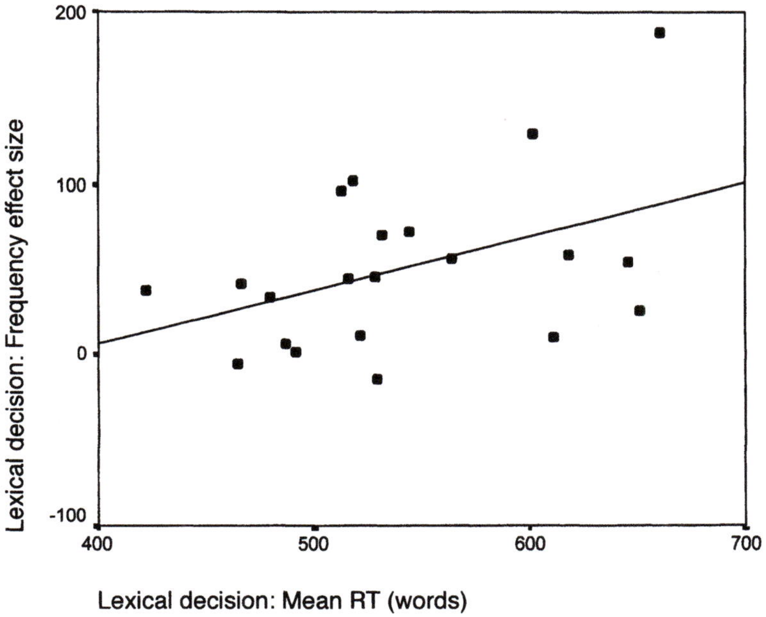


(ii) Lexical decision & imageability

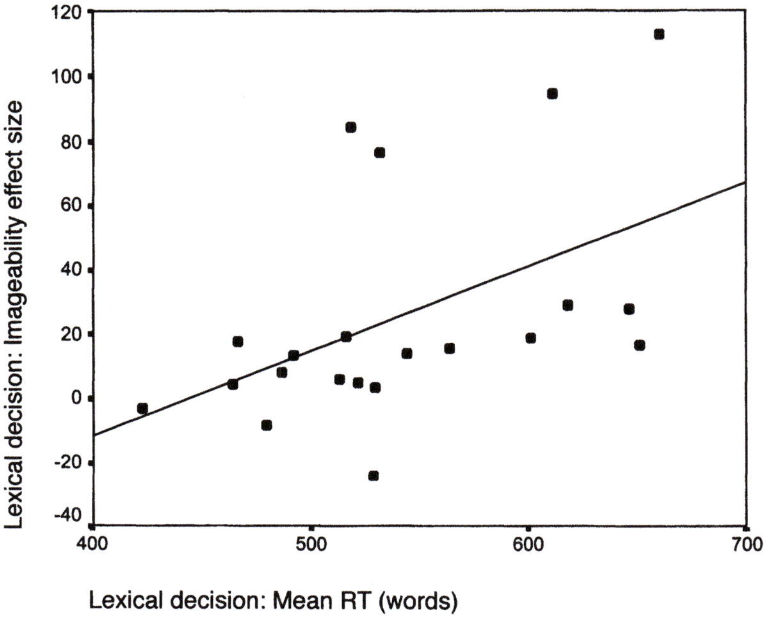

(iii) Homophone judgements: Regular and exception words

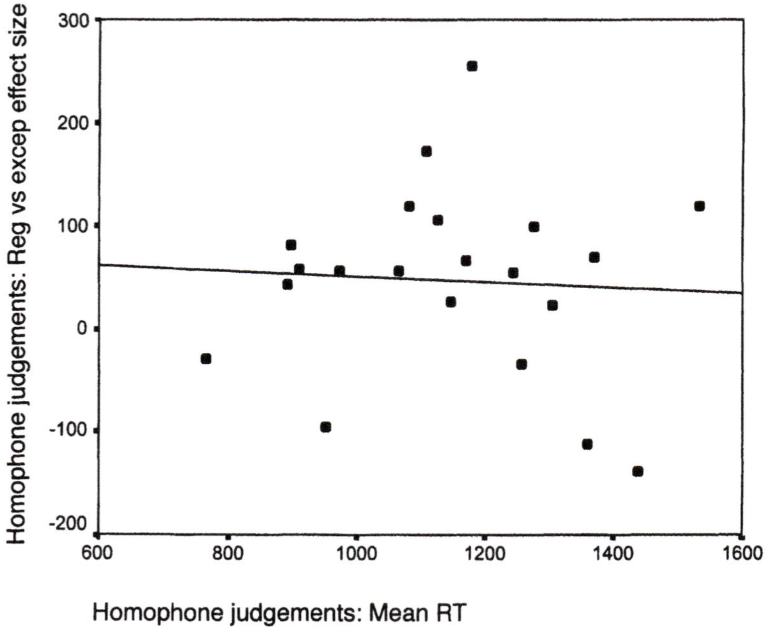


(iv) Homophone judgements: Regular vs nonwords

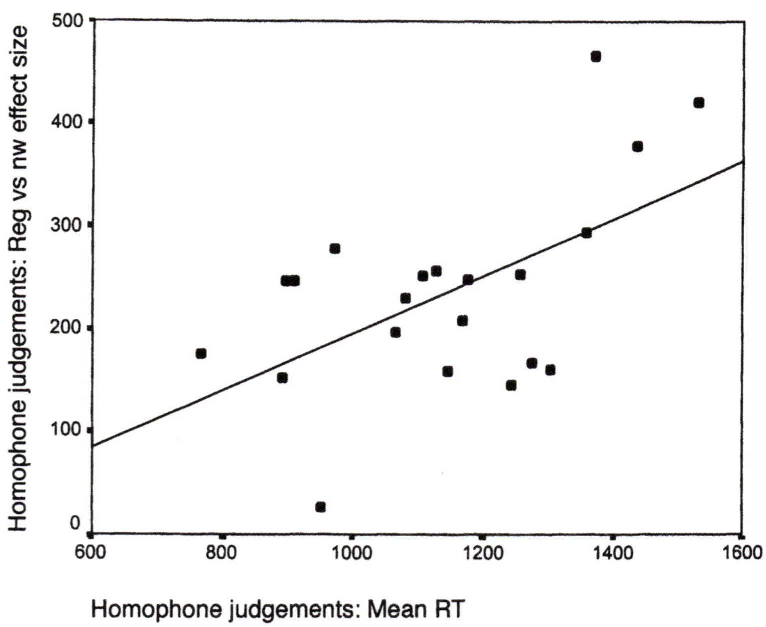

(v) Homophone judgements: Exception vs nonwords

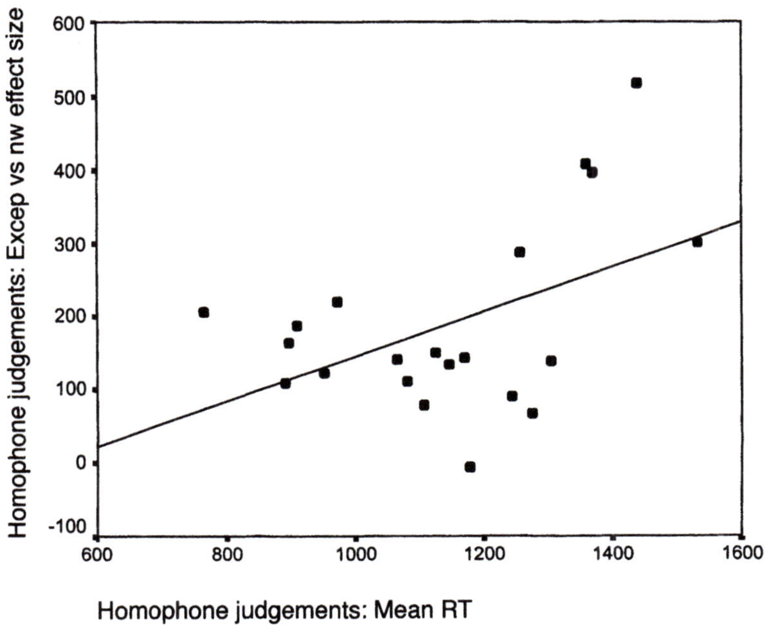


(vi) Rhyme judgements: Effect of rhyme

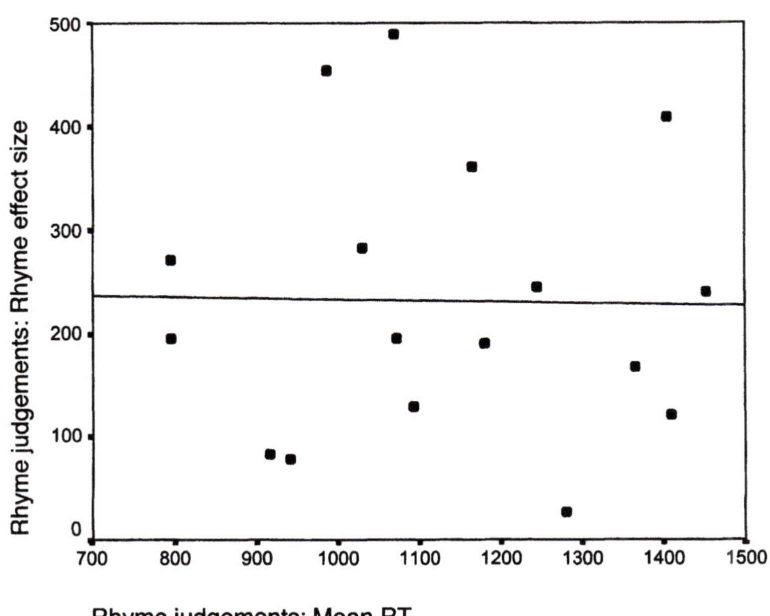

(vii) Rhyme judgements: Effects of visual similarity

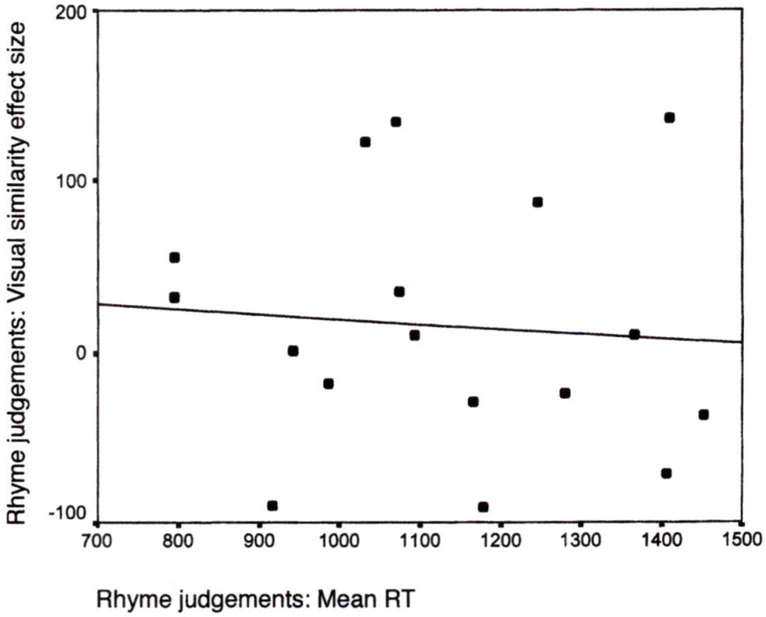

APHASIOLOGY, 2004, *18* (2), 127–151

# Review

# Ten years on: Lessons learned from published studies that cite the PALPA

Janice Kay and Richard Terry
*University of Exeter, UK*

*Background*: This paper presents a review of the use of the PALPA (Kay, Lesser, & Coltheart, 1992) in published research studies in which it is cited.
*Aims*: In an examination of annual citation counts from 1991 to 2001, the review aims to discover the journals in which the PALPA has been most frequently cited, the frequency of citation, and the country of origin of the cited article. It also explores the design of studies (e.g., single case, case series, group), the nature of the aetiology of the patients tested, and the topic areas investigated (e.g., investigations of theory, rehabilitation or neuroimaging studies). In particular, the review explores the frequency with which particular tests have been used and suggests reasons why some are used more than others.
*Main Contribution*: The review considers reasons why some tests in the PALPA have proved to be more popular than others. These lead to conclusions about its experimental use over the past decade and, in particular, to how development of the battery should proceed in any future revision.
*Conclusions*: The review reveals that PALPA has a consistent and continued high citation rate, suggesting that it has been sufficiently well received by researchers across related fields within aphasiology for it to be used as an assessment and research tool, and that it is still found to be useful even 10 years after its introduction. It is observed that some tests are cited more widely than others, leading to conclusions about their effectiveness in research studies. While use of PALPA in a clinical setting is not considered, thereby limiting conclusions about applicability, the paper also provides information of value to clinicians, especially with regard to the detailed analysis of why certain tests have been used more often than others.

1992 saw the publication of a new collection of tests designed to be a resource for researchers and clinicians wishing to assess the language-processing abilities of people with aphasia. The PALPA (Psycholinguistic Assessments Of Language Processing in Aphasia; Kay, Lesser, & Coltheart, 1992) was constructed in response to the authors' own experiences of aphasia research and aphasia rehabilitation programmes. They had identified a need for a comprehensive "off-the-peg" collection of language-processing tests that would provide researchers and clinicians with the means to carry out detailed investigations of language-processing impairments in people with acquired brain damage, and to establish baseline performance and allow comparisons to be drawn across

Address correspondence to: Janice Kay, University of Exeter, Washington Singer Labs, Exeter EX4 4QG, UK. Email: j.m.kay@exeter.ac.uk

The authors would like to thank Chris Code, Max Coltheart, Matt Lambon Ralph, and especially Lyndsey Nickels and Brendan Weekes for their help in completing this review.


http://www.tandf.co.uk/journals/pp/02687038.html DOI:10.1080/02687030344000490

individual cases. Since its publication in English, PALPA has been translated and adapted for use in a number of different languages and there are now Spanish (Valle & Cuetos, 1995), Dutch (Bastiaanse, Bosje & Visch-Brink, 1995), and Hebrew (Gil & Edelstein, 2001) versions.

PALPA consists of 60 assessments. The tests are arranged in four separate sections: *Auditory Processing*, *Reading and Spelling*, *Word and Picture Semantics*, and *Sentence Processing*. A fifth section provides an introduction to the battery, with details about how the tests were constructed and the theoretical framework that underpins them. Following a cognitive neuropsychological approach, this framework assumes a componential structure of language-processing abilities, such as producing a spoken name in response to a picture, or writing down a dictated word. PALPA aims to provide precision tools for the systematic diagnosis of which components of the system may be impaired. It is designed to allow the investigator (researcher and/or clinician) to pinpoint precisely, by a process of hypothesis testing, what is impaired in language processing, and what remains relatively preserved. Control data are provided with some, but not all, tests, against which to judge impairment (Kay, Lesser, & Coltheart, 1996). The fact that not all tests include normative data is a weakness that is discussed further in Section 4 of this paper.

In this paper, we set out to investigate, some 10 years after publication, to what extent PALPA has constituted a useful tool for clinicians and researchers, and what its limitations have been. Our approach to these questions has been to seek to provide a detailed analysis of use of PALPA tests in studies published over the past decade. This approach is, of course, necessarily limited, because it can provide few insights into actual use of the battery (in the clinic, for example), but only as it has been used and reported in experimental and clinical research.

For a more clinically based account of PALPA's use see Horton and Byng, 2001; Katz et al., 2000. In a survey of clinical test use in five healthcare systems in Australia, Canada, the UK, and the US, PALPA was the most frequently used in routine UK assessment of acute aphasic inpatients and chronic aphasic outpatients, although the Boston Diagnostic Aphasia Examination (Goodglass & Kaplan, 1973, 1982; Western Aphasia Battery (Kertesz, 1982), and the Boston Naming Test (Kaplan, Goodglass, & Weintraub, 1983) appeared to be the most frequently used regardless of healthcare system (Katz et al., 2000).

By carrying out a review of published studies that cite PALPA, we hope to give an indication of its success (or otherwise) in light of the authors' aspirations to provide a flexible and practical resource for assessment of acquired language disorders. We also intend it to be the first step in a planned revision of the battery. From our own experience and that of other researchers, it seems likely some tests have been more widely used than others; our search identifies such tests, discusses why they may have been more popular and the implications for less popular tests.

## INVESTIGATING PALPA'S USE: A CITATIONS-BASED APPROACH

This paper presents a review of journal articles that have cited PALPA over the period from its publication in 1992 until 2002 (pre-publication citations for 1991 have also been included). Some 218 separate articles were identified following two cited reference searches using the ISI Web of Science database (conducted in July 2001 and April 2002). A total of 216 articles were acquired in hard copy (it was not possible to obtain two articles), providing the raw materials on which the review is based. It should be noted that, while every effort was made to ensure that the citations search was as comprehensive as possible, it only yielded hits for English-language publications. In addition, it remains possible that a number of articles may have been missed by the search.

A variety of information was extracted from each paper and collated to provide the data summarised in this report: quantitative, qualitative, and descriptive. The review is arranged in four sections. Section 1 sets out the demography of PALPA's citations over the decade; that is, the number and frequency of citations and the journals in which they appear. Section 2 looks in more detail at the nature of the studies that are described in the papers: the type of study, the area of investigation, and the broad aetiology of the patients involved in the studies. Section 3 examines descriptive data on the frequency of use of individual tests, and includes a more detailed discussion of some of the more frequently used tests, including information on how they have been used and other batteries/tests that have been used in conjunction with them. Section 4 summarises the conclusions about PALPA's experimental use over the past decade and discusses implications for a future revision, including our own views and those of colleagues in the field.

## 1. ANALYSES OF CITATION COUNT

### 1.1 Citation count by year

When did the articles that cite PALPA appear?[1] Figure 1 shows that the number of studies citing PALPA has risen steadily since its publication. Despite a slight downturn in the late 1990s, it continues to generate a high number of citations today. For comparison, Figures 2 and 3 illustrate citation figures for the Pyramids and Palm Trees Test (Howard & Patterson, 1992) and the Birmingham Object Recognition Battery (Riddoch &

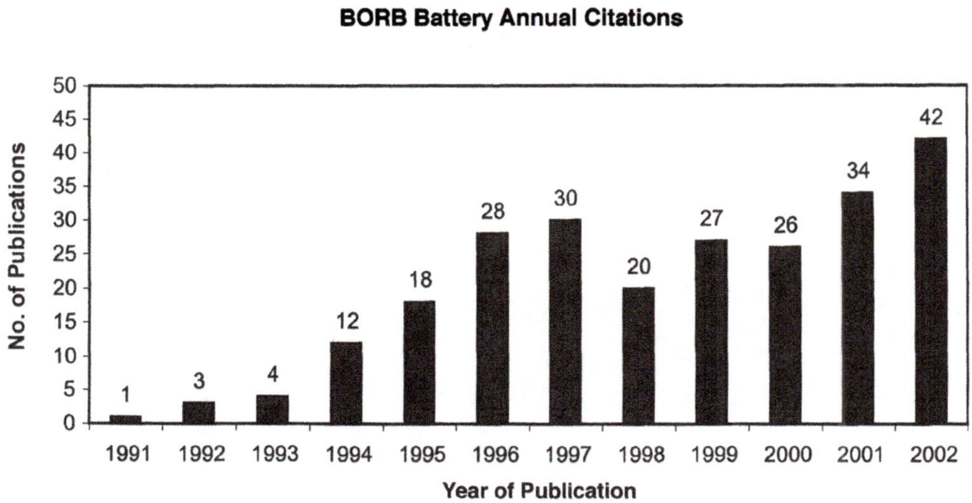


**Figure 1.** PALPA citations by year.

[1] Note that the citation count for 2002 reflects the total as indicated by a further citation search conducted in April 2003. This search indicated an additional 29 citations (raising the citations total to 245). However, only 13 of the 42 articles published in 2002 were available at the time of the analyses described in Sections 2 and onwards of this report.

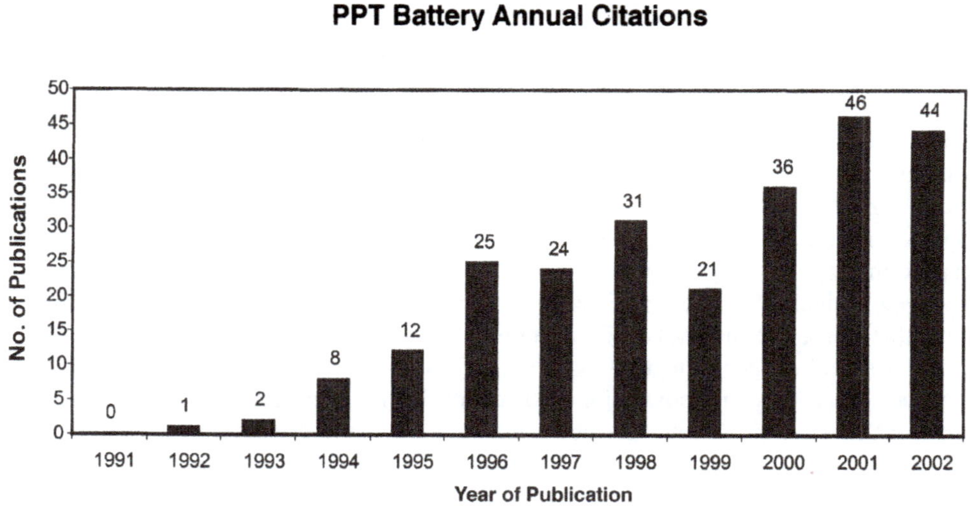


**Figure 2.** Pyramid and Palm Trees Test citations by year.

Humphreys, 1993). A very similar profile, including the slight downturn in the late 1990s, can be seen for these assessments.

PALPA's consistent and continued high citation rate indicates that the battery has been sufficiently well received by researchers across related fields of language impairment for it to be used as an assessment and research tool, and that it is still found to be useful even 10 years after its introduction.[2]

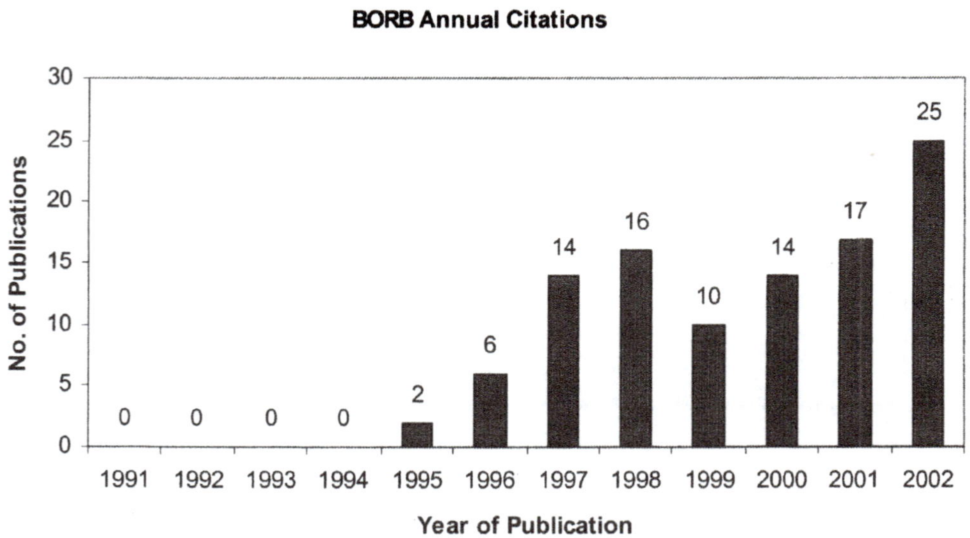


**Figure 3.** Birmingham Object Recognition Battery citations by year.

[2] The battery was published at the end of 1992, but Figure 1 includes citations from 1991 when unpublished versions of the test were available.

## 1.2 Citations by country of origin

Table 1 shows the geographical spread of PALPA citations as indicated by the base of the first author. Perhaps not surprisingly for a battery published first in the UK, 90% of the citations are drawn from studies by authors working in predominantly English-speaking countries (UK, USA, Australia, Canada, & New Zealand). Most of the researchers are based in the UK, reflecting the prominence of the cognitive neuropsychological approach in Britain and consistent with the publicity that heralded its arrival and that it continues to receive there. There are fewer citations by researchers in the USA, perhaps reflecting the fact that there are some pictorial and linguistic differences that inevitably restrict its use (e.g., tap/faucet), the more widespread use of standardised aphasia batteries (e.g., Boston Diagnostic Aphasia Examination; Goodglass & Kaplan, 1972, 1983) and alternative materials (e.g., Johns Hopkins Dyslexia and Dysgraphia Battery).

Data can be found about those cases in which PALPA has been translated/adapted for use in other languages. For example, four out of the five citations from Spanish authors use the Spanish version of PALPA (Cuetos & Ellis, 1999; Cuetos & Labos, 2001; Cuetos, Valle-Arroyo & Suarez, 1996; Dieguez-Vide, Bohm, Gold, Roch-Lecours, & Pena-Casanova, 1999). The Dutch version of PALPA was cited three times, twice in studies by German authors (de Bleser, Faiss, & Schwarz, 1995; de Bleser, Reul, Kotlarek, Faiss, & Schwartz, 1994) and once in a Dutch paper (Bastiaanse, Bosje, & Franssen, 1996). The Hebrew version, published in 2001, was cited twice, both times in studies by the same Israeli author (Friedmann, 2002; Friedmann & Gvion, 2001). In the remaining citations from other authors (those from Denmark, Germany, France, Netherlands, Belgium, Italy, and Singapore), all but two involved the use of the English-language version of PALPA (for example, in comparative testing in studies involving bilinguals). The two exceptions were studies by Danish authors in which selected tests from the English-language version of PALPA were translated on an ad-hoc basis for use with Danish participants (Jensen, 2000; Pedersen, Vinter, & Olsen, 2001).

TABLE 1
Geographical spread of PALPA citations

| *Country of origin* | *1991* | *1992* | *1993* | *1994* | *1995* | *1996* | *1997* | *1998* | *1999* | *2000* | *2001* | *2002* | *Totals* |
|---|---|---|---|---|---|---|---|---|---|---|---|---|---|
| UK | 1 | 3 | 4 | 7 | 14 | 16 | 23 | 12 | 15 | 16 | 20 | 8 | 139 |
| USA | – | – | 1 | 1 | 2 | 4 | 6 | 5 | 5 | 5 | 4 | 1 | 34 |
| Australia | – | – | – | 2 | – | 2 | – | – | 1 | 1 | 6 | 1 | 13 |
| Canada | – | – | – | 1 | – | 1 | 1 | – | 1 | 3 | – | – | 7 |
| Spain | – | – | – | – | – | 1 | – | – | 2 | – | 2 | – | 5 |
| Germany | – | – | – | 1 | 1 | – | – | 1 | 1 | – | – | – | 4 |
| France | – | – | – | – | 1 | 1 | – | 1 | – | – | – | – | 3 |
| New Zealand | – | – | – | – | – | 1 | – | – | – | – | – | 2 | 3 |
| Denmark | – | – | – | – | – | – | – | – | – | 1 | 1 | – | 2 |
| Israel | – | – | – | – | – | – | – | – | – | – | 1 | 1 | 2 |
| Netherlands | – | – | – | – | – | 1 | – | – | 1 | – | – | – | 2 |
| Belgium | – | – | – | – | – | 1 | – | – | – | – | – | – | 1 |
| Italy | – | – | – | – | – | – | – | – | 1 | – | – | – | 1 |
| Singapore | – | – | – | – | – | – | – | 1 | – | – | – | – | 1 |
| Total studies | 1 | 3 | 5 | 12 | 18 | 28 | 30 | 20 | 27 | 26 | 34 | 13 | 217 |

Country of origin (first author) of studies citing PALPA – year by year.

Although there are only a few translations/adaptations of the complete PALPA assessments, it is worth noting that its approach has encouraged adaptation of critical tests, such as written word–picture matching and reading aloud of regular and irregular words. This, in turn, has resulted in significant new knowledge about language processing in those languages (see, for example, Law & Orr, 2001; Reich, Chou, & Patterson, 2003; Weekes & Chen, 1999; Weekes, Davies, Parris, & Robinson, 2003, with regard to written word processing in Chinese).

## 1.3 Citations by journal

Over the publication period, PALPA citations have appeared in 48 different publications. Table 2 indicates the total number and frequency of citations, in ranked order with the journals most frequently citing PALPA at the top. The right-hand column of the table shows the percentage share of the total citations by publication.

A total of 56% (121) of citations come from mainstream neuropsychological journals. Nonetheless, it should also be noted that PALPA has been cited in articles appearing in a number of more specialised publications such as *Current Biology* (Varley & Siegal, 2000), *Epileptic Disorders* (Sieratzki, Calvert, Brammer, David, & Woll, 2001), and *Human Brain Mapping* (Herbster, Mintun, Nebes & Becker, 1997), and has also been cited in two articles in *Nature* (Marslen-Wilson & Tyler, 1997; Scott, Young, Calder, Hellawell, Aggleton, & Johnson, 1997).

The wide range of publications in which PALPA citations occur reflects the potential applications of the battery and suggests that, while its most popular uses are those for which it was primarily developed (i.e., as a neuropsychological assessment tool, and as a specialist battery probing language impairments), it is also flexible enough to provide applications beyond those for which it was designed (e.g., for use in development and testing of rehabilitation/therapy programmes). This can be seen more clearly in analyses of the nature of cited studies (in Section 2 of this paper).

Analysis was also carried out on citation count by journal by year. *Aphasiology* appeared as one of the three journals with highest PALPA citations for 9/11 years of the count,[3] and *Cognitive Neuropsychology* for 7/11 years (overall, *Cognitive Neuropsychology* has the highest percentage share). *Neurocase* appears in the count in 1996, its first year of publication, but also carries the third highest citation rate overall. As would be expected within this collection of journals, many (generally mainstream neuropsychological journals such as *Cognitive Neuropsychology*) tend to have high ISI Journal Citation Impact Factors (a score of 1 or above).[4] This suggests that the battery remains a popular tool amongst high-calibre researchers and research groups.

[3] This may reflect the use of PALPA by clinical researchers who choose this journal as a vehicle for their work and may possibly reflect a trend to include PALPA in the development and monitoring of rehabilitation/therapy programmes, reports of which tend to be well covered in this publication (see Section 2.2 later).

[4] According to the ISI website "the journal impact factor is a measure of the frequency with which the 'average article' in a journal has been cited in a particular year. The impact factor is calculated by dividing the number of current citations to articles published in the two previous years by the total number of articles published in the two previous years".

TABLE 2
Frequency of PALPA citations by journal

| *%age share* | *Totals (ranked all years)* | *Publication* |
|---|---|---|
| 18.06 | 39 | *Cognitive Neuropsychology* |
| 16.67 | 36 | *Aphasiology* |
| 8.33 | 18 | *Neurocase* |
| 6.94 | 15 | *Brain & Language* |
| 6.02 | 13 | *Neuropsychologia* |
| 5.56 | 12 | *Journal of Neurolinguistics* |
| 5.09 | 11 | *International Journal of Language and Communication Disorders* |
| 3.24 | 7 | *Cortex* |
| 2.78 | 6 | *Quarterly Journal of Experimental Psychology* |
| 2.31 | 5 | *Neuropsychological Rehabilitation* |
| 1.85 | 4 | *Journal of Cognitive Neuroscience* |
| 1.85 | 4 | *Journal of the International Neuropsychological Society* |
| 1.39 | 3 | *Journal of Neurology* |
| 0.93 | 2 | *Applied Psycholinguistics* |
| 0.93 | 2 | *Brain* |
| 0.93 | 2 | *Brain and Cognition* |
| 0.93 | 2 | *International Journal of Psychophysiology* |
| 0.93 | 2 | *Journal of Experimental Psychology: Human Perception and Performance* |
| 0.93 | 2 | *Journal of Memory and Language* |
| 0.93 | 2 | *L'Année Psychologique* |
| 0.93 | 2 | *Memory* |
| 0.93 | 2 | *Nature* |
| 0.93 | 2 | *Neurorehabilitation and Neural Repair* |
| 0.46 | 1 | *Aging & Mental Health* |
| 0.46 | 1 | *Brain Injury* |
| 0.46 | 1 | *British Journal of Hospital Medicine* |
| 0.46 | 1 | *British Journal of Psychiatry* |
| 0.46 | 1 | *British Journal of Psychology* |
| 0.46 | 1 | *Clinical Linguistics & Phonetics* |
| 0.46 | 1 | *Current Biology* |
| 0.46 | 1 | *Disability & Rehabilitation* |
| 0.46 | 1 | *Epileptic Disorders* |
| 0.46 | 1 | *Experimental Brain Research* |
| 0.46 | 1 | *Human Brain Mapping* |
| 0.46 | 1 | *Journal of Child Psychology & Psychiatry* |
| 0.46 | 1 | *Journal of Head Trauma Rehabilitation* |
| 0.46 | 1 | *Journal of Medical Speech-Language Pathology* |
| 0.46 | 1 | *Journal of Speech, Language and Hearing Research* |
| 0.46 | 1 | *Journal of the Acoustical Society of America* |
| 0.46 | 1 | *Journal of the Neurological Sciences* |
| 0.46 | 1 | *Language & Cognitive Processes* |
| 0.46 | 1 | *Lingua* |
| 0.46 | 1 | *Proceedings of the Royal Society, London B* |
| 0.46 | 1 | *Psychological Review* |
| 0.46 | 1 | *Revue Européene de Psychologie Appliquée* |
| 0.46 | 1 | *Seminars in Neurology* |

Ranked citation hit rate – all journals 1991–2002.

## 2. NATURE OF STUDIES CITED

### 2.1 Design of studies

While the tests in the PALPA were designed to help in the assessment of acquired language processing difficulties of individuals, its use has not been restricted to single case approaches. As Table 3 shows, while 50% (109) of PALPA citations are reports of single cases, a considerable number make use of larger samples. Note that the table is arranged to show by year the number of experimental investigations, therapy studies, and brain-imaging studies. Omitted from this table are 18 theoretical/review articles and 4 book reviews. For simplicity of classification, "single case" refers to studies that report the performance of a single individual (see, for example, Forde, Francis, Riddoch, Rumiati, & Humphreys, 1997; Hanley, Davies, Downes, & Mayes, 1994), "case series" indicates studies of between two and four individuals (Snowden, Griffiths & Neary, 1996; Hirsh & Funnell, 1995), and "larger case series" refers to reports of five or more individuals (Annett, Eglinton, & Smythe, 1996; Nickels & Howard, 1994). Where we use the term "case series control study", this refers to papers in which the performance of between two and four clinical cases is contrasted directly with that of a number of control participants (see, for example, Mummery, Ashburner, Scott, & Wise, 1999), and "larger case series control study" refers to reports involving five or more clinical cases and controls (e.g., James, van Steenbrugge, & Chiveralls, 1994). Nickels (2002) distinguishes between different kinds of case series designs but, as numbers of each type are quite small, we have not done so here.

While the majority of citations of experimental work (78%) consist of experimental investigations, therapy studies constitute the next largest group (17.5%), followed by brain-imaging studies (4.5%). Single cases are the most popular design, although proportionately more citations featuring PALPA consist of case series reports in later years.[5] This may parallel methodological development in cognitive neuropsychology in which the single case study approach that dominated the 1980s and early 1990s is now accompanied by case series designs and group studies, particularly in brain imaging and in work that makes use of patients with more constrained neurological impairment (e.g., in semantic dementia).

### 2.2 Topic area

This section looks in more detail at the topic areas addressed by these studies. These data were analysed by year (see Table 3) and it can be observed how the relative frequency of therapy-based citations increased from 1999 onwards. Two journals account for 68% of these citations, 20 (55%) are from *Aphasiology* and 5 (13%) are from *International Journal of Language and Communication Disorders.*

It is of interest to note the variety of different theoretical areas PALPA has been used to investigate (see Table 4). Investigations of aphasia account for most of the citations, with spoken word production and visual word recognition and reading aloud being the most widely explored of the subject areas. This is perhaps unsurprising in the case of reading, since PALPA developed from a series of tests designed to investigate acquired disorders of reading and spelling (29 tests, almost half of the collection). There are also a

[5] In the five years between 1992 and 1996, single case studies were the subject of 41/53 (77%) of citations, falling to 84/122 (69%) between 1997 and 2001.

TABLE 3
Design of studies

| *Nature of study* | *No. of NCP* | *1991* | *1992* | *1993* | *1994* | *1995* | *1996* | *1997* | *1998* | *1999* | *2000* | *2001* | *2002* | *Total* |
|---|---|---|---|---|---|---|---|---|---|---|---|---|---|---|
| Single case | 1 | – | 3 | 2 | 8 | 10 | 14 | 16 | 9 | 12 | 14 | 16 | 5 | 109 |
| Case series study | 2 to 4 | – | – | – | – | 2 | 5 | 3 | 3 | 2 | 2 | 2 | – | 19 |
| Larger case series | 5 or over | – | – | – | 1 | 1 | – | 1 | 1 | 1 | – | 1 | 3 | 9 |
| Case series control | 2 to 4 | – | – | – | – | – | 1 | 1 | – | – | – | – | – | 2 |
| Larger case series control study | 5 or over | – | – | – | 1 | – | 2 | 2 | 1 | 2 | – | 1 | 3 | 12 |
| Therapy study – single case | 1 | 1 | – | 1 | – | – | 3 | 3 | 2 | 2 | 4 | 3 | – | 19 |
| Therapy study – case series study | 2 to 4 | – | – | – | 1 | 1 | – | – | 2 | 1 | 1 | 3 | 1 | 10 |
| Therapy study – larger case studies | 5 or over | – | – | 1 | – | – | – | – | – | 1 | – | 1 | – | 3 |
| Therapy study – larger case studies control | 5 or over | – | – | – | – | – | – | – | – | – | – | 2 | – | 2 |
| Neuroimaging/ERP/TMS – single case | 1 | – | – | – | 1 | – | – | – | – | 1 | – | 2 | – | 4 |
| Neuroimaging/ERP/TMS – group study | 2 to 4 | – | – | – | – | – | – | 1 | – | – | 1 | – | – | 2 |
| Neuroimaging/ERP/TMS – control study | 2 to 4 | – | – | – | – | – | – | 1 | – | 1 | – | 1 | – | 3 |
| Theoretical/Review article | n/a | – | – | – | – | 3 | 3 | 2 | 2 | 2 | 3 | 2 | 1 | 18 |
| Book review | n/a | – | – | – | – | 1 | – | – | – | 2 | 1 | – | – | 4 |
| Total studies | | 1 | 3 | 4 | 12 | 18 | 28 | 30 | 20 | 27 | 26 | 34 | 13 | 216 |

Nature of studies citing PALPA – year by year.
NCP: Non-control participants.

TABLE 4
Topics of study

| | |
|---|---|
| *Investigations of theory* | |
| Object and face processing | 8 |
| Visual perception and movement | 3 |
| Attentional systems | 2 |
| Visual word recognition and reading aloud | 27 |
| Auditory word processing | 9 |
| Language and the right hemisphere | 4 |
| Structure of semantic memory | 24 |
| Spoken word production | 32 |
| Development and language | 10 |
| Written and oral spelling | 10 |
| Reading, spelling and phonology | 6 |
| Memory and amnesia | 2 |
| Syntactic processing | 11 |
| Emotional processing | 1 |
| Frontal lobe disorders | 2 |
| *Therapy studies* | |
| Treatments for acquired reading disorders | 7 |
| Treatments for auditory processing disorders | 4 |
| Treatments for semantic comprehension disorders | 2 |
| Treatments for word-finding disorders | 12 |
| Treatments for acquired spelling disorders | 6 |
| Treatments for syntactic disorders | 2 |
| Training for carers | 1 |
| *Neuro-imaging studies* | 9 |
| *Total* | 194 |

relatively large number of PALPA citations from studies looking at semantic memory and category-specific disorders. This may reflect the popularity of PALPA Picture and Word Semantic tests (e.g., tests [47] & [48])[6] as a tool for probing semantic memory impairment (these two tests featured in 9 of the 14 studies that considered this topic area) and we shall return to discuss the use of particular tests in a later section. It may also reflect the proliferation of studies in this area (e.g., Martin & Caramazza, 2003).

## 2.3 Patient aetiology

The aetiology of patients with whom the PALPA was used in cited studies was also analysed (see Table 5). Some studies (41) did not provide the reader with precise information about aetiology or neurological damage, or described patients with mixed aetiologies (classified as Undisclosed or Other in Table 5). The remainder could be classified by aetiology, either without localising information, with primary or predominant right or left hemisphere damage, bilateral damage, or as developmental data.

The table shows that PALPA has been used with patients with a variety of aetiologies. The principal group is patients with left hemisphere acquired brain damage, although it has been used with right hemisphere and bilateral patients and with

[6] Numbers in square brackets indicate PALPA test number, from [1] to [60].

TABLE 5
Aetiology

| | |
|---|---|
| *Aetiology non-localised* | |
| CVA | 23 |
| Dementias | 11 |
| Encephalitis, incl herpes simplex | 2 |
| Acquired brain injury, incl RTA | 1 |
| Brain tumour | 1 |
| Progressive supranuclear palsy | 1 |
| Motor neurone disease | 1 |
| Schizophrenia | 1 |
| Genetic disorder/epilepsy | 1 |
| Sub-total | 42 |
| *Primary/predominant left hemisphere* | |
| CVA | 92 |
| Lesion | 12 |
| Dementias | 7 |
| Acquired brain injury, incl RTA | 4 |
| Meningitis | 1 |
| Sub-total | 116 |
| *Primary/predominant right hemisphere* | |
| CVA | 6 |
| Dementias | 1 |
| Encephalitis incl herpes simplex | 1 |
| Hemispherectomy | 1 |
| Undisclosed aetiology | 1 |
| *Sub-total* | 10 |
| *Bilateral lesion* | 4 |
| *Developmental* | 3 |
| *Undisclosed/Other* | 41 |
| *Total* | 216 |

developmental cases (it should be emphasised, however, that the collection of tests is designed for use with people with acquired disorders, who are assumed to have been competent users of language; PALPA does not include any developmental norms). The majority (121 or 56%) of reports describe patients with CVA, most of whom have had left hemisphere damage (within this category, primary location of damage varies: left parietal, temporal, thalamic etc.), and a smaller number with RH disorder (as Table 5 shows, in some cases localising information is not provided). Progressive degenerative conditions, summarised as Dementias in the table, are the next most common group, accounting for 9% of citations. These conditions include non-fluent progressive dysphasia and fluent progressive dysphasia (semantic dementia), as well as dementia of Alzheimer type. There are a few studies whose participants have presented with other conditions such as encephalitis, principally herpes simplex viral encephalitis (e.g., Tyler, de Mornay-Davies, Anokhina, Longworth, Randall, & Marslen-Wilson, 2002), motor neurone disease (e.g., Cobble, 1998), epilepsy (e.g., Humphreys & Riddoch, 1999), and schizophrenia (e.g., Edelstyn, Oyebode, Riddoch, Soppitt, Moselhy, & George, 1997).

# 3. USE OF INDIVIDUAL PALPA TESTS

## 3.1 Identifying most and least popular tests

By examining in detail the papers that cite PALPA, we were able to gather data on which tests had been used and how they had been used. Tables 6 to 9 illustrate frequency of use of each of the 60 tests. The tables are organised by the type of test and the section in which it is found: Auditory Processing, Reading and Spelling, Picture and Word Semantics, and Sentence Comprehension. The results are ranked, with the most commonly used tests first. Note that, in some cases, the description is not detailed enough to allow us to identify the specific sub-test (e.g., by its number). In these cases, we have either noted the kind of test (e.g., "Unspecified Auditory Processing Test") or the level (e.g., "Unspecified Minimal Pairs Task"). Note that these data are not ranked, but shown at the bottom of the tables.

Consonant with instructions about how PALPA should be used, it is clear that the collection of tests is not used in its entirety. In fact, it is rare that tests that constitute a particular section are used together, although examples do exist (e.g., Kiran, Thompson, & Hashimoto, 2001; Tree, Perfect, Hirsh, & Copstick, 2002). In these cases, tests are usually those from the Reading and Spelling or Picture and Word Semantics sections.

Table 10 classifies usage of tests as either "initial" or "primary". Initial test use represents a record of those occasions in which a test has been employed (usually in the context of a number of other tests) to assess the status of broad areas of language processing (i.e., to assess auditory processing abilities in the context of an overall neuropsychological assessment). Primary test use, on the other hand, represents a record of

TABLE 6
Citation frequency of auditory processing tests

| *Battery* | *Test no.* | *Test name* | *Times used* |
|---|---|---|---|
| Auditory Processing | 5 | Auditory/Lexical Decision: Imag × Freq | 27 |
| Auditory Processing | 2 | Word Minimal Pairs | 15 |
| Auditory Processing | 8 | Repetition: Nonwords | 15 |
| Auditory Processing | 1 | Nonword Minimal Pairs | 12 |
| Auditory Processing | 15 | Rhyme Judgements × Words | 10 |
| Auditory Processing | 9 | Repetition: Imag × Freq | 8 |
| Auditory Processing | 13 | Digit Production/Matching Span | 8 |
| Auditory Processing | 7 | Repetition: Syllable Length | 7 |
| Auditory Processing | 4 | Word Minimal Pairs Requiring Picture Selection | 5 |
| Auditory Processing | 3 | Word Minimal Pairs Requiring Written Selection | 3 |
| Auditory Processing | 14 | Rhyme Judgements × Pictures | 3 |
| Auditory Processing | n/a | Unspecified Minimal Pairs Task | 2 |
| Auditory Processing | 12 | Repetition: Sentences | 2 |
| Auditory Processing | n/a | Unspecified Repetition Task | 2 |
| Auditory Processing | 16 | Phonological Segmentation: Initial Sounds | 2 |
| Auditory Processing | 6 | Auditory Lexical Decision: Morphological Endings | 1 |
| Auditory Processing | n/a | Unspecified Auditory Lexical Decision | 1 |
| Auditory Processing | 10 | Repetition: Grammatical Class | 1 |
| Auditory Processing | 17 | Phonological Segmentation: Final Sounds | 1 |
| Auditory Processing | 11 | Repetition: Morphological Endings | 0 |
| Auditory Processing | Unspecified | Unspecified | 6 |
| | | Totals | 131 |

TABLE 7
Citation frequency of reading and spelling tests

| *Battery* | *Test no.* | *Test name* | *Times used* |
|---|---|---|---|
| Reading & Spelling | 36 | Oral Reading: Nonwords | 39 |
| Reading & Spellling | 31 | Oral Reading: Imag × Freq | 28 |
| Reading & Spelling | 24 | Visual Lexical Decision: Legality | 24 |
| Reading & Spelling | 35 | Oral Reading: Regularity | 23 |
| Reading & Spelling | 25 | Visual Lexical Decision: Imag × Freq | 20 |
| Reading & Spelling | 19 | Letter Discrimination: Upper > Lower Case Matching | 17 |
| Reading & Spelling | 20 | Letter Discrimination: Lower > Upper Case Matching | 17 |
| Reading & Spelling | 28 | Homophone Decision | 14 |
| Reading & Spelling | 29 | Oral Reading: Letter Length | 14 |
| Reading & Spelling | 30 | Oral Reading: Syllable Length | 14 |
| Reading & Spelling | 32 | Oral Reading: Grammatical Class | 14 |
| Reading & Spelling | 44 | Spelling to Dictation: Regularity | 12 |
| Reading & Spelling | 18 | Letter Discrimination: Mirror Reversal | 10 |
| Reading & Spelling | 22 | Letter Naming & Sounding | 10 |
| Reading & Spelling | 23 | Spoken Letter – Written Letter Matching | 10 |
| Reading & Spelling | 27 | Visual Lexical Decision: Regularity | 10 |
| Reading & Spelling | 40 | Spelling to Dictation: Imag × Freq | 8 |
| Reading & Spelling | 45 | Spelling to Dictation: Nonwords | 8 |
| Reading & Spelling | 39 | Spelling to Dictation: Letter Length | 7 |
| Reading & Spelling | 33 | Oral Reading: Grammatical Class × Imag | 6 |
| Reading & Spelling | 34 | Oral Reading: Morphological Endings | 5 |
| Reading & Spelling | 38 | Homophone Definition × Regularity | 4 |
| Reading & Spelling | 41 | Spelling to Dictation: Grammatical Class | 3 |
| Reading & Spelling | 42 | Spelling to Dictation: Grammatical Class × Imag | 3 |
| Reading & Spelling | 43 | Spelling to Dictation: Morphological Endings | 3 |
| Reading & Spelling | 26 | Visual Lexical Decision: Morphological Endings | 2 |
| Reading & Spelling | n/a | Unspecified Letter Discrimination | 1 |
| Reading & Spelling | 37 | Oral Reading: Sentences | 1 |
| Reading & Spelling | n/a | Unspecified Oral Reading | 1 |
| Reading & Spelling | 46 | Spelling to Dictation: Disambiguated Homophones | 1 |
| Reading & Spelling | n/a | Unspecified Spelling to Dictation | 1 |
| Reading & Spelling | 21 | Letter Discrimination: Words & Nonwords | 0 |
| Reading & Spelling | Unspecified | Unspecified | 10 |
| | | Totals | 340 |

those occasions in which a test has been given (often in isolation, or with a smaller number of other tests) to investigate in more detail the nature of a specific impairment (i.e., to assess whether a patient has a particular difficulty in reading aloud exception words in the context of investigating an acquired reading disorder such as surface dyslexia). Even in these cases, however, researchers have generally also devised their own experimental materials to test key theoretical predictions.

Although PALPA tests have been used both as initial and primary materials, there is a small bias towards their usage as initial tests in preliminary assessment prior to carrying out further experimental investigations of language processing. Although PALPA was designed as an assessment rather than experimental tool, it is gratifying to see that it is sufficiently flexible to be used for broad-based assessments in neuropsychological evaluations of language and as a more precise instrument for use in isolating and exploring more specific neuropsychological impairments in detail.

TABLE 8
Citation frequency of picture and word semantics

| *Battery* | *Test no.* | *Test name* | *Times used* |
|---|---|---|---|
| Picture & Word Semantics | 47 | Spoken Word – Picture Matching | 89 |
| Picture & Word Semantics | 48 | Written Word – Picture Matching | 84 |
| Picture & Word Semantics | 49 | Auditory Synonym Judgements | 27 |
| Picture & Word Semantics | 50 | Written Synonym Judgements | 18 |
| Picture & Word Semantics | 53 | Picture Naming × Written Naming/Repetition/Oral Reading/Written Spelling | 18 |
| Picture & Word Semantics | n/a | Unspecified Picture Matching Task | 13 |
| Picture & Word Semantics | 51 | Word Semantic Association | 12 |
| Picture & Word Semantics | 54 | Picture Naming × Frequency | 12 |
| Picture & Word Semantics | 52 | Spoken Word – Written Word Matching | 6 |
| Picture & Word Semantics | n/a | Unspecified Picture Naming Task | 4 |
| Picture & Word Semantics | n/a | Unspecified Synonym Judgement Task | 2 |
| Picture & Word Semantics | Unspecified | Unspecified | 1 |
| | | Totals | 286 |

Across all of the citations, PALPA tests were described in 797 instances. Of these, 438 (55%) were as initial tests, compared to 359 (45%) as primary tests. (It is perhaps worth noting at this point that these figures may underestimate the research use of individual tests, as papers that report important follow-up studies may have relied on PALPA tests for initial assessment and diagnosis, but do not reference them further.) This applies consistently across sections, except for the Reading and Spelling tests, where the trend is reversed (see Table 8): 55% of the reported instances of use are as primary tests. However, closer inspection of the data shows that this results from just two oral reading tests: Nonwords [24] & Imageability × Frequency [31]. This may be because these two tests in particular have proved useful, in combination with other tasks, in exploring the nature of underlying impairments in acquired dyslexia, rather than just in assessing the nature of the condition. They are well matched, control data are supplied, and they can be used across modality (e.g., auditory versions exist). Several authors (see, for example, Hanley, Hastie, & Kay, 1992; Ogden, 1996) have used these tests to explore further orthographic and phonological processing in surface dyslexia and phonological dyslexia, for example.

TABLE 9
Citation frequency of sentence processing tests

| *Battery* | *Test no.* | *Test name* | *Times used* |
|---|---|---|---|
| Sentence Comprehension | 55 | Auditory Sentence Comprehension | 10 |
| Sentence Comprehension | 56 | Written Sentence Comprehension | 10 |
| Sentence Comprehension | 57 | Auditory Comprehension of Verbs & Adjectives from the Sentence Set | 3 |
| Sentence Comprehension | 58 | Auditory Comprehension of Locative Relations | 1 |
| Sentence Comprehension | 59 | Written Comprehension of Locative Relations | 0 |
| Sentence Comprehension | 60 | Pointing Span for Noun – Verb Sequences | 0 |
| Sentence Comprehension | Unspecified | Unspecified | 3 |
| | | Totals | 27 |

Subtracting 33 instances in which we were unable to identify the particular test, we are left with 764 test citations. Table 10 reviews the data presented in Tables 6 to 9 in a way that allows us to identify the frequency of use of each test, ranked in order of overall popularity. The table allows for the easy identification of clear "favourites", and, at the bottom of the list, a number of tests that have not been used in published studies that we have identified. Three types of test have enjoyed regular use: semantic matching, reading aloud, and lexical decision. All of the 8 Picture and Word Semantics tests feature in the top 25 most-used tasks. More importantly, 2 of them, Spoken Word–Picture Matching [47] and its sister version, Written Word–Picture Matching [48], account for 173 citations, nearly one quarter (24%) of all reported instances of test use. Of their use, 66% has been as an initial test assessment, suggesting, perhaps, that they are popular as general tests of semantic functioning.

TABLE 10
Ranked frequency of cited test use

| *Battery* | *Test no.* | *Test name* | *Times used* | *Initial* | *Primary* |
|---|---|---|---|---|---|
| Picture & Word Semantics | 47 | Spoken Word – Picture Matching | 89 | 59 | 30 |
| Picture & Word Semantics | 48 | Written Word – Picture Matching | 84 | 55 | 29 |
| Reading & Spelling | 36 | Oral Reading: Nonwords | 39 | 15 | 24 |
| Reading & Spelling | 31 | Oral Reading: Imag × Freq | 28 | 7 | 21 |
| Auditory Processing | 5 | Auditory Lexical Decision: Imag × Freq | 27 | 15 | 12 |
| Picture & Word Semantics | 49 | Auditory Synonym Judgements | 27 | 16 | 11 |
| Reading & Spelling | 24 | Visual Lexical Decision Legality | 24 | 13 | 11 |
| Reading & Spelling | 35 | Oral Reading: Regularity | 23 | 14 | 9 |
| Reading & Spelling | 25 | Visual Lexical Decision: Imag × Freq | 20 | 9 | 11 |
| Picture & Word Semantics | 50 | Written Synonym Judgements | 18 | 9 | 9 |
| Picture & Word Semantics | 53 | Picture Naming × Written Naming/ Repetition/Oral Reading/Written Spelling | 18 | 12 | 6 |
| Reading & Spelling | 19 | Letter Discrimination: Upper > Lower Case Matching | 17 | 11 | 6 |
| Reading & Spelling | 20 | Letter Discrimination: Lower > Upper Case Matching | 17 | 10 | 7 |
| Auditory Processing | 2 | Word Minimal Pairs | 15 | 10 | 5 |
| Auditory Processing | 8 | Repetition: Nonwords | 15 | 8 | 7 |
| Reading & Spelling | 28 | Homophone Decision | 14 | 8 | 6 |
| Reading & Spelling | 29 | Oral Reading: Letter Length | 14 | 7 | 7 |
| Reading & Spelling | 30 | Oral Reading: Syllable Length | 14 | 7 | 7 |
| Reading & Spelling | 32 | Oral Reading: Grammatical Class | 14 | 7 | 7 |
| Picture & Word Semantics | n/a | Unspecified Picture Matching Task | 13 | 9 | 4 |
| Auditory Processing | 1 | Nonword Minimal Pairs | 12 | 7 | 5 |
| Reading & Spelling | 44 | Spelling to Dictation: Regularity | 12 | 4 | 8 |
| Picture & Word Semantics | 51 | Word Semantic Association | 12 | 8 | 4 |
| Picture & Word Semantics | 54 | Picture Naming × Frequency | 12 | 8 | 4 |
| Auditory Processing | 15 | Rhyme Judgements × Words | 10 | 7 | 3 |
| Reading & Spelling | 18 | Letter Discrimination: Mirror Reversal | 10 | 3 | 7 |
| Reading & Spelling | 22 | Letter Naming & Sounding | 10 | 5 | 5 |
| Reading & Spelling | 23 | Spoken Letter – Written Letter Matching | 10 | 5 | 5 |
| Reading & Spelling | 27 | Visual Lexical Decision: Regularity | 10 | 2 | 8 |
| Sentence Comprehension | 55 | Auditory Sentence Comprehension | 10 | 6 | 4 |

(Continued)

TABLE 10
(Continued)

| Battery | Test no. | Test name | Times used | Initial | Primary |
|---|---|---|---|---|---|
| Sentence Comprehension | 56 | Written Sentence Comprehension | 10 | 5 | 5 |
| Auditory Processing | 9 | Repetition: Imag × Freq | 8 | 3 | 5 |
| Auditory Processing | 13 | Digit Production/Matching Span | 8 | 6 | 2 |
| Reading & Spelling | 40 | Spelling to Dictation: Imag × Freq | 8 | 4 | 4 |
| Reading & Spelling | 45 | Spelling to Dictation: Nonwords | 8 | 3 | 5 |
| Auditory Processing | 7 | Repetition: Syllable Length | 7 | 4 | 3 |
| Reading & Spelling | 39 | Spelling to Dictation: Letter Length | 7 | 3 | 4 |
| Reading & Spelling | 33 | Oral Reading: Grammatical Class × Imag | 6 | 1 | 5 |
| Picture & Word Semantics | 52 | Spoken Word – Written Word Matching | 6 | 4 | 2 |
| Auditory Processing | 4 | Word Minimal Pairs Requiring Picture Selection | 5 | 2 | 3 |
| Reading & Spelling | 34 | Oral Reading: Morphological Endings | 5 | 2 | 3 |
| Reading & Spelling | 38 | Homophone Definition × Regularity | 4 | 1 | 3 |
| Picture & Word Semantics | n/a | Unspecified Picture Naming Task | 4 | 1 | 3 |
| Auditory Processing | 3 | Word Minimal Pairs Requiring Written Selection | 3 | 2 | 1 |
| Auditory Processing | 14 | Rhyme Judgements × Pictures | 3 | 2 | 1 |
| Reading & Spelling | 41 | Spelling to Dictation: Grammatical Class | 3 | 0 | 3 |
| Reading & Spelling | 42 | Spelling to Dictation: Grammatical Class × Imag | 3 | 1 | 2 |
| Reading & Spelling | 43 | Spelling to Dictation: Morphological Endings | 3 | 1 | 2 |
| Sentence Comprehension | 57 | Auditory Comprehension of Verbs & Adjectives from the Sentence Set | 3 | 3 | 0 |
| Auditory Processing | n/a | Unspecified Minimal Pairs Task | 2 | 1 | 1 |
| Auditory Processing | 12 | Repetition: Sentences | 2 | 2 | 0 |
| Auditory Processing | n/a | Unspecified Repetition Task | 2 | 2 | 0 |
| Auditory Processing | 16 | Phonological Segmentation: Initial Sounds | 2 | 2 | 0 |
| Reading & Spelling | 26 | Visual Lexical Decision: Morphological Endings | 2 | 1 | 1 |
| Picture & Word Semantics | n/a | Unspecified Synonym Judgement Task | 2 | 2 | 0 |
| Auditory Processing | 6 | Auditory Lexical Decision: Morphological Endings | 1 | 0 | 1 |
| Auditory Processing | n/a | Unspecified Auditory Lexical Decision | 1 | 0 | 1 |
| Auditory Processing | 10 | Repetition: Grammatical Class | 1 | 0 | 1 |
| Auditory Processing | 17 | Phonological Segmentation: Final Sounds | 1 | 1 | 0 |
| Reading & Spelling | n/a | Unspecified Letter Discrimination | 1 | 0 | 1 |
| Reading & Spelling | 37 | Oral Reading: Sentences | 1 | 0 | 1 |
| Reading & Spelling | n/a | Unspecified Oral Reading | 1 | 1 | 0 |
| Reading & Spelling | 46 | Spelling to Dictation: Disambiguated Homophones | 1 | 0 | 1 |
| Reading & Spelling | n/a | Unspecified Spelling to Dictation | 1 | 1 | 0 |
| Sentence Comprehension | 58 | Auditory Comprehension of Locative Relations | 1 | 0 | 1 |
| Auditory Processing | 11 | Repetition: Morphological Endings | 0 | 0 | 0 |
| Reading & Spelling | 21 | Letter Discrimination: Words & Nonwords | 0 | 0 | 0 |
| Sentence Comprehension | 59 | Written Comprehension of Locative Relations | 0 | 0 | 0 |
| Sentence Comprehension | 60 | Pointing Span for Noun – Verb Sequences | 0 | 0 | 0 |

Subtest use rank order by test – all years

The next two most popular tests are two oral reading tests: Nonwords [24] & Imageability × Frequency [31]. A further oral reading test of word regularity [35] also scores highly and, between them, these three tests account for 11% of all reported instances of PALPA test use. As we mentioned earlier, it seems likely that these tests feature prominently because of their use in differentiating different kinds of acquired dyslexic disorder. It is also worth noting in this context that the fifth test in the list is the auditory lexical decision version [5] of the Imageability × Frequency reading aloud test [31]. Along with the written lexical decision version [25], ninth in the list, these tasks have clearly showed their worth in exploring impairments that may be frequency and/or imageability dependent within and across modality.

Four tests were not cited at all. Two of them, Written Comprehension of Locative Relations [59] and Pointing Span for Noun–Verb Sequences [60] are from the Sentence Comprehension tests. Of the four PALPA manuals, this one has received the least favourable reviews (Basso, 1996; Marshall, 1996), and it may be the case that at least some of the tests in this manual are better suited to experimental investigation of syntactic processing than to diagnostic assessment. In addition, there exists a well-recognised clinical alternative, namely the Test for Reception of Grammar (TROG; Bishop, 1983), which, though designed to assess developmental conditions, can equally highlight acquired difficulties in written and auditory syntactic comprehension. Experimentally, other tests are available, such as Schwartz, Saffran, and Marin's (1980) reversible sentences (see also Marshall, Black, & Byng, 1999).

Two other tests, Repetition: Morphological Endings [11] and Letter Discrimination: Words & Nonwords [21] were also not cited, which may also reflect the fact that neither of them has particular value as a diagnostic tool, and they were designed more with experimental investigation of auditory processing and orthographic analysis in mind. In fact, an identical letter discrimination task has been used to investigate the acquired dyslexic disorder of letter-by-letter reading, although this has always been in the format of a reaction-time task (e.g., Behrmann, Nelson & Sekuler, 1998; Kay & Hanley, 1991; Reuter-Lorenz & Brunn, 1990).

As the four sections do not contain an equal number of tests, it is perhaps not appropriate simply to look at the raw frequencies of cited usage for each collection of tests. A more equitable approach is to weight the data according to the number of tests in each section before considering the relative contribution each has made to PALPA's overall use. After such weightings have been applied, the most popular of the four sections in terms of cited use is the Picture & Word Semantics tests, accounting for some 61% of all instances. Next comes Reading & Spelling tests (19.5%), tests of Auditory Processing (12.5%) and, finally, Sentence Comprehension tests (7%).

## 3.2 Tests of picture and word semantics

The most popular test in the entire collection, Spoken Word–Picture Matching [47] has tended to find use more as an initial assessment tool of semantic impairment. Even within this domain, however, there has been considerable variation in the ways in which it has been applied, and the specific areas of function that it has been used to probe. For example, some studies have used the test to investigate semantic access impairments (e.g., Marshall, Pring, Chiat, & Robson, 2001; Weekes, Coltheart, & Gordon, 1997), while others have used it as a more general gauge of the extent to which semantic comprehension remains intact (e.g., Beaton, Guest, & Ved, 1997; Graham, Lambon Ralph, & Hodges, 1997; Kay & Hanley, 1999; Kay, Hanley, & Miles, 2001; Patterson &

Behrmann, 1997). It is popularly administered as part of the diagnosis of overall cognitive performance, prior to further investigation (e.g., Forde & Humphreys, 1997; Howard, Best, Bruce, & Gatehouse, 1995; Snowden et al., 1996). Several studies have included it in assessments given both before and after programmes of aphasia therapy (e.g., Hinckley, Patterson, & Carr, 2001; Kiran et al., 2001), so that it serves as a measure of the efficacy of the treatment given. Other studies have used this test to assess cognitive functions that are not directly related to semantic processing, for example, the test has been used in studies to assess baseline levels of lexical (e.g., Hall & Riddoch, 1998; Spencer, Doyle, McNeil, Wambaugh, Park, & Caroll, 2000) and object processing (e.g., Harris, Harris, & Caine, 2001; Scarna & Ellis, 2002).

As a primary test, it has been used to explore specific hypotheses about the nature of semantic processing (e.g., Best, 1995; Forde & Humphreys, 1995; Lambon Ralph, Ellis, & Franklin, 1995; Lambon Ralph, Sage, & Ellis, 1996). For example, Nickels and Howard (1994) used it to check that errors made in a picture-naming task given to a group of aphasic patients were indeed semantic errors and could not be attributed to visual errors—the test contains not only semantically related (and not visually related) distractors, but also those that are only visually related, and others that are semantically and visually related. Maneta, Marshall, and Lindsay (2001) applied the test as an assessment of sound discrimination abilities following therapy in an aphasic individual with word-sound deafness. They reasoned that if discrimination had improved as a result of their therapeutic intervention, then it may have improved the patient's access to word semantics from auditory input.

We were interested to discover which tests were employed in combination with the Spoken Word–Picture Matching task. The Pyramids and Palm Trees Test (PPT) (Howard & Patterson, 1992) has been used the most extensively (37% of studies citing use of Spoken Word–Picture Matching have also administered the PPT). Other test batteries that have co-occurred include the Boston Naming Test (BNT, Kaplan et al., 1983) in 13% of reported studies, the Birmingham Object Recognition Battery (BORB, Riddoch & Humphreys, 1993), and the Test for Reception of Grammar (TROG, Bishop, 1983), which both feature in 9% of those studies citing the use of PALPA 47. There are other similar available tests (e.g., spoken word–picture naming test from the ADA Battery, Franklin, Turner, & Ellis, 1992, which uses distractors that are phonologically related to the target word). This is, of course, of benefit to the researcher who is able to compare performance across tasks with similar format but generally different items.

It should come as little surprise to find that use of Written Word–Picture Matching [48] is very similar to that of Test 47, given that 85% of all the reported instances come from studies where both tests were applied in tandem. In fact, there were only 13 cited examples in which the written word version was used on its own, and these tended to be with cases where the primary focus is on reading impairment (e.g., Funnell, 1996; Gerhand, McCaffer & Barry, 2000). In most studies, both versions of the test were employed to compare the status of semantic comprehension using the semantic matching (between picture and word) and the same materials, either in spoken word or written word form. The Pyramids and Palm Trees test, and related Camel and Cactus test (Bozeat et al., 2003) make use of semantic association judgements and can therefore examine lexical semantic processing of spoken and written words (e.g., three written word or spoken word, two written word version), and conceptual processing of pictures (three picture version), as well as spoken word–picture association.

A recent study by Cole-Virtue and Nickels (2004 this issue) has examined the structure of materials of the Word–Picture Matching tests [47 & 48] and has demonstrated some confounds between the distractors. In particular, the authors report that the semantic and visually related distractors are more closely related to the target than the semantic but not visually related distractors, showing that more errors on the former set is not a reliable marker of additional visual perceptual difficulty. Nonetheless, the authors conclude that the tests reliably distinguish semantic comprehension impairments.

Auditory and written synonym judgements [49] and [50] also appear to be well used (both within the 10 most frequently cited tasks), even though normative data are not provided (as with some others in the battery). Nickels and Cole-Virtue (2004 this issue) present reaction-time and accuracy data from young controls on the synonym judgement tasks (and on homophone, rhyme, and visual lexical decision tasks). It is important that a revision of the battery should include normative data for all tasks (this point is considered in the final section). PALPA includes two picture-naming tasks. One (Picture Naming: Oral and Written Naming, Repetition, Oral Reading, Written Spelling [53]) has proved to be more cited than the other (Picture Naming: Frequency [54]) and this may be because the former also encourages testing across different tasks and modalities, and/or because the latter does not include picture materials—they are taken from the Snodgrass and Vanderwart (1980) stimuli—and/or some other factor.

## 3.3 Tests of reading and spelling

There are six letter discrimination tasks in PALPA, two of which have been cited relatively frequently (cross-case matching [18] & [19]), three less often (mirror reversal [20], letter naming and sounding [21] & [22], and spoken letter–written letter matching [23]) and one not at all (letter discrimination in words and nonwords [21]). As has been discussed, the latter test is of most use with a reaction-time format and, even though it may have a specific role in assessment of peripheral acquired reading disorders such as pure alexia and letter-by-letter reading, and associated impairments of visual processing (e.g., Behrmann et al., 1998), lack of citations show that this use has not been realised. If this particular letter discrimination task is to find a place in a revision, there would need to be clearer instructions about the conditions in which it should be employed. Letter naming and sounding tasks are straightforward to construct and researchers generally use their own materials. Even though the mirror reversal test has been cited 10 times, this has generally been to show that impairments of this ability are not present (there are only rare examples of mirror reading in the literature; e.g., Lambon Ralph, Jarvis, & Ellis, 1997), and one can reasonably question whether this should have a place in the revised battery. Certainly, 6 of 60, or 10% of tasks, concerned with letter discrimination, is probably too many.

Visual lexical decision tasks that have employed "legal" and "illegal" nonwords [24] or words of high and low imageability and frequency [25] are frequently cited (within the top 10), while a similar task that makes use of different morphological endings [26] was cited only twice. Homophone decision [28] is also well cited, although two other homophone tasks barely feature ([38] and [46]). Oral reading tasks have generally proved to be popular: six out of eight have featured in the top twenty. Reading tasks tend to be cited more often than spelling versions (spelling tests are generally constructed from the reading tasks, but contain fewer items). This may be because reading tasks have been found to be more useful, or because studies of acquired dyslexia are more frequent in the literature (we speculate that the former is the more likely, as studies of acquired dysgraphia have tended to employ alternative materials, such as the Johns Hopkins Dysgraphia Battery). Linked with this possibility, we note that the PALPA test of regularity in spelling [44] uses a subset of the words constructed from the test of regularity in oral reading [35]. There are more irregularities in spelling than in reading in English, which is why only a subset was used for testing spelling (to ensure that, as far as possible, the regular words really did have regular and predictable spellings). However, with more sophisticated statistical datasets of spelling alternatives for particular sounds now available (e.g. Ziegler, Stone, & Jacobs, 1997), it is possible that researchers may have preferred to construct their own tests of sound–spelling regularity. A future revision of PALPA should take this factor into account.

## 3.4 Tests of auditory processing

Four auditory processing tasks feature in the top 20 most frequently cited tasks: Auditory Lexical Decision: Imageability and Frequency [5], Word Minimal Pairs [2], Repetition of Nonwords [8], and Nonword Minimal Pairs [1]. We have noted the usefulness of repeating items, and indeed tasks, across modality and this undoubtedly contributes to the use of the auditory lexical decision task. Word and nonword minimal pairs have tended to be used together in assessments of auditory processing, as they were designed to be. Note that there are complementary sets of stimuli in the ADA Battery (Franklin et al., 1992), which also include "maximally different" pairs (see also Morris, Franklin, Ellis, Turner, & Bailey, 1996). To judge from citations, Word Minimal Pairs Requiring Picture Selection [4] has proved less useful; this may be because of difficulties in interpreting some of the picture materials (which may also apply to the Rhyme Judgements with Pictures task [14]). Of least use in this section appear to have been the phonological segmentation tasks [16] and [17], arguably because their format is not only too complex, but also because they are not "pure" segmentation tasks. The tests require segmentation of a phoneme from a heard word and a match to be made with a corresponding written letter. Failure may follow from working memory demands and visual impairments as well as from phonological difficulties. A revision should make use of segmentation and blending tasks such as those constructed by Patterson and Marcel (1992), and others, which are designed to tap phonological skills with minimal memory load.

## 3.5 Tests of sentence comprehension

As we discussed above, tests of sentence comprehension have been cited least often. Collectively, three of the six tests in this section were cited only once. This appears not just to be because there are alternative assessments such as the TROG (Bishop, 1982) (we have noted that it is an advantage to have a number of available tests with which to examine the robustness of an impairment), but because the format and structure of the tasks are often too complex, and may be prone to experimental confounds. Also, the section does not include an assessment of sentence production. At the same time, however, it is should be emphasised that these conclusions are based on cited use in research studies and has not taken into account ways in which they may have been used clinically.

# 4. LESSONS FOR A FUTURE REVISION

Our examination of the number of citations that PALPA has received in the years since its publication in 1992 suggests that it has been relatively well used and that there are no indications thus far that its use is declining. We have identified more and less popular tests according to cited use, and speculated on why this may have been the case. One reason contributing to low popularity is undoubtedly lack of normative data, although this by itself does not seem to have prevented tests being used: Auditory and Written Synonym Judgement tasks, for example, are among the most popular but do not include norms. Nonetheless, we suggest that a revision of the battery should include normative data for all tests. As the battery has been employed not only with older adults with acquired brain damage, but with younger adults, and children and adolescents in developmental studies, age-appropriate data are required.

That some tests have not been cited indicates that they have not been helpful assessment tools, at least when measured by citations in research journals (although note that the corollary does not hold: they may have been useful in clinical assessment). We have suggested that there may be a variety of reasons why this could be the case. While it is clear that some of them are simply not very good tests, others may have been used less frequently because they have more selective applications. This may suggest that there should be an explicit distinction between those tests that have a more general applicability, perhaps as ''core'' tests, and those that have a more selective function, perhaps as ''supplementary'' tasks. Some, if not all, ''core'' tests could also be flagged as having particular relevance in screening. Indicating which tests could be used as screening assessments would also serve to reduce the time taken to formulate a profile of performance, and would be more appropriate (and methodologically adequate) than simply cutting down the number of items given. It is important to emphasise the perils of not giving a particular test in its entirety. The tests are not designed to be given in a truncated form and will not therefore reveal effects of particular variables (e.g., imageability, frequency) reliably if presented in this way.

There are examples where this design principle of using the same materials across modality is not followed, but perhaps should be for best effect. For instance, it would be useful if comprehension and production tasks such as Spoken Word–Picture Matching and Picture Naming employed the same materials. There are other examples of tests that should be included in a revision of the battery because their importance has been highlighted in more recent experimental findings. Thus, age-of-acquisition has been shown in recent studies to be an important variable in spoken word retrieval (e.g., Morrison & Ellis, 1995) and in reading and spelling (e.g., Weekes et al., 2003) and should therefore be included in selection of picture naming, and reading and spelling materials. However, this needs to be achieved through maintaining a key strength of PALPA, which is that items are matched carefully (as far as possible on a one-to-one basis) for particular variables, even in control sets, while the variable of interest is manipulated.

We recognise, too, that tests of auditory-verbal short-term memory also need to be developed further. The same applies to tests of action naming as well as object naming and comprehension, since PALPA picture materials have tended to focus principally on noun categories. New empirical findings also change advice in the battery about ''where to go next'' in selecting assessment tests. For example, recent work on the nature of surface dyslexia suggests the importance of assessing semantic processing skills, as well as phonological abilities in reading regular and irregular words (e.g., Patterson & Hodges, 1992).

Our review of published articles that cite PALPA shows that it constitutes a useful set of tools with which to assess language-processing impairments. It has been used to investigate a wide variety of disorders, with people with different aetiologies. Detailed examination of individual tests has revealed which have been most used, and those less used. We suggest that such data will provide input into a future revision of the battery, although we also note other factors, such as provision of normative data, which must be included if the battery is to reach its full potential in aphasiological research and assessment.

## REFERENCES


Annett, M., Eglinton, E., & Smythe, P. (1996). Types of dyslexia and the shift to dextrality. *Journal of Child Psychology & Psychiatry*, *37*, 167–180.

Basso, A. (1996). PALPA: An appreciation and a few criticisms. *Aphasiology*, *10*, 190–193.

Bastiaanse, R., Bosje, M., & Franssen, M. (1996). Deficit-oriented treatment of word-finding problems: Another replication. *Aphasiology*, *10*, 363–383.

Bastiaanse, R., Bosje, M., & Visch-Brink, E. (1995). *PALPA, Nederlandse Versie*. Hove, UK: Lawrence Erlbaum Associates Ltd.

Beaton, A., Guest, J., & Ved, R. (1997). Semantic errors of naming, reading, writing, and drawing following left-hemisphere infarction. *Cognitive Neuropsychology*, *14*, 459–478.

Behrmann, M., Nelson, J., & Sekuler, E. B. (1998). Visual complexity in letter-by-letter reading: "Pure" alexia is not pure. *Cognitive Neuropsychology*, *12*, 409–454.

Best, W. (1995). A reverse length effect in dysphasic naming: When elephant is easier than ant. *Cortex*, *31*, 637–652.

Bishop, D. V. M. (1983). *The Test for Reception of Grammar*. Published by the author and available from Age and Cognitive Performance Research Centre, University of Manchester, M13 9PL, UK.

Bozeat, S., Lambon Ralph, M. A., Graham, K., Patterson, K., Wilkin, H., Rowland, J. et al. (2003). A duck with four legs: Investigating the structure of conceptual knowledge using picture drawing in semantic dementia. *Cognitive Neuropsychology*, *20*, 27–47.

Cobble, M. (1998). Language impairment in motor neurone disease. *Journal of the Neurological Sciences*, *160*, 47–52.

Cole-Virtue, J., & Nickels, L. (1004). Spoken word to picture matching from PALPA: A critique and some new matched sets. *Aphasiology*, *18*, 77–102.

Cuetos, F., & Ellis, A. W. (1999). Visual paralexias in a Spanish-speaking patient with acquired dyslexia: A consequence of visual and semantic impairments? *Cortex*, *35*, 661–647.

Cuetos, F., & Labos, E. (2001). The autonomy of the orthographic pathway in a shallow language: Data from an aphasic patient. *Aphasiology*, *15*, 333–342.

Cuetos, F., Valle-Arroyo, F., & Suarez, M. (1996). A case of phonological dyslexia in Spanish. *Cognitive Neuropsychology*, *13*, 1–24.

De Bleser, R., Faiss, J., & Schwarz, M. (1995). Rapid recovery of aphasia and deep dyslexia after cerebrovascular left-hemisphere damage in childhood. *Journal of Neurolinguistics*, *9*, 9–22.

De Bleser, R., Reul, J., Kotlarek, F., Faiss, C., & Schwartz, M. (1994). Rapid recovery of aphasia and deep dyslexia after extensive left-hemisphere damage in childhood. *Brain & Language*, *47*, 474–476.

Dieguez-Vide, F., Bohm, P., Gold, D., Roch-Lecours, A., & Pena-Casanova, J. (1999). Acquired dyslexias and dysgraphias (II): Clinical protocol for the assessment of reading and writing disorders in Spanish. *Journal of Neurolinguistics*, *12*, 115–146.

Edelstyn, N. M. J., Oyebode, F., Riddoch, M. J., Soppitt, R., Moselhy, H., & George, M. (1997). A neuropsychological perspective on three schizophrenic patients with midline structural defects. *British Journal of Psychiatry*, *170*, 416–421.

Forde, E. M. E., Francis, D., Riddoch, M. J., Rumiati, R. I., & Humphreys, G. W. (1997). On the links between visual knowledge and naming: A single case of a patient with a category-specific impairment for living things. *Cognitive Neuropsychology*, *14*, 403–458.

Forde, E., & Humphreys, G. W. (1995). Refractory semantics in global aphasia: On semantic organisation and the access-storage distinction in neuropsychology. *Memory*, *3*, 265–307.

Forde, E. M. E., & Humphreys, G. W. (1997). A semantic locus for refractory behaviour: Implications for access-storage distinctions and the nature of semantic memory. Cognitive *Neuropsychology*, *14*, 367–402.

Franklin, S., Turner, J. E., & Ellis, A. W. (1992). *The ADA Comprehension Battery*. York, UK: University of York Human Neuropsychology Laboratory.

Friedmann, N. (2002). Question production in agrammatism: The tree pruning hypothesis. *Brain & Language*, *80*, 160–187.

Friedmann, N., & Gvion, A. (2001) Letter position dyslexia. *Cognitive Neuropsychology*, *18*, 673–696.

Funnell, E. (1996). Response biases in oral reading: An account of the co-occurrence of surface dyslexia and semantic dementia. *The Quarterly Journal of Experimental Psychology*, *49*A, 417–446.

Gerhand, S., McCaffer, F., & Barry, C. (2000). Surface or deep dyslexia? A report of a patient who makes both regularization and semantic errors in oral reading. *Neurocase*, *6*, 393–401.

Gil, M., & Edelstein, C. (2001). *Hebrew version of the PALPA*. Ra'anana, Israel: Loewenstein Hospital Rehabilitation Center.

Goodglass, H., & Kaplan, E. (1973). *Boston Diagnostic Aphasia Examination.* Philadelphia: Lea & Febiger.
Goodglass, H., & Kaplan, E. (1982). *Boston Diagnostic Aphasia Examination* (2nd ed.). Philadelphia: Lea & Febiger.
Graham, K. S., Lambon Ralph, M. A., & Hodges, J. R. (1997). Determining the impact of autobiographical experience on ''meaning'': New insights from investigating sports-related vocabulary and knowledge in two cases with semantic dementia. *Cognitive Neuropsychology, 14,* 801–837.
Hall, D. A., & Riddoch, M. J. (1998). Word meaning deafness: Spelling words that are not understood. *Cognitive Neuropsychology, 14,* 1131–1164.
Hanley, J. R., Davies, A. D. M., Downes, J. J., & Mayes, A. R. (1994). Impaired recall of verbal material following rupture and repair of an anterior communicating artery aneurism. *Cognitive Neuropsychology, 11,* 543–578.
Hanley, J. R., Hastie, K., & Kay, J. (1992). Developmental surface dyslexia and dysgraphia: An orthographic processing impairment. *The Quarterly Journal of Experimental Psychology, 44*A, 285–319.
Harris, I. M., Harris, J. A., & Caine, D. (2001). Object orientation agnosia: A failure to find the axis? *Journal of Cognitive Neuroscience, 13,* 800–812.
Herbster, A. N., Mintun, M. A., Nebes, R. D., & Becker, J. T. (1997). Regional cerebral blood flow during word and nonword reading. *Human Brain Mapping, 5,* 84–92.
Hinckley, J. J., Patterson, J. P., & Carr, T. H. (2001). Differential effects of context-and-skill based treatment approaches: Preliminary findings. *Aphasiology, 15,* 463–476.
Hirsh, K. W., & Funnell, E. (1995). Those old, familiar things: Age of acquisition, familiarity and lexical access in progressive aphasia. *Journal of Neurolinguistics, 9,* 23–32.
Horton, S., & Byng, S. (2001). Examining interaction in language therapy. *International Journal of Language and Communication Disorders, 30,* 86–91.
Howard, D., Best, W., Bruce, C., & Gatehouse, C. (1995). Operativity and animacy effects in aphasic naming. *European Journal of Disorders of Communication, 30,* 286–302.
Howard, D., & Patterson, K. E. (1992). *The Pyramids and Palm Trees Test.* Bury St. Edmunds, UK: Thames Valley Test Company.
Humphreys, G. W., & Riddoch, M. J. (1999). Impaired development of semantic memory: Separating semantic from structural knowledge and diagnosing a role for action in establishing stored memories for objects. *Neurocase, 5,* 519–532.
James, D., Van Steenbrugge, W., & Chiveralls, K. (1994). Underlying deficits in language-disordered children with central auditory processing difficulties. *Applied Psycholinguistics, 15,* 311–328.
Jensen, L. R. (2000). Canonical structure without access to verbs? *Aphasiology, 14,* 827–850.
Kaplan, E., Goodglass, H., & Weintraub, S. (1983). *Boston Naming Test.* Philadelphia: Lea & Febiger.
Katz, R. C., Hallowell, B., Code, C., Armstrong, E., Roberts, P., Pounds, C. et al. (2000). A multinational comparison of aphasia management practice. *International Journal of Language and Communication Disorders, 35,* 303–314.
Kay, J., & Hanley, R. (1991). Simultaneous form perception and serial letter recognition in a case of letter-by-letter reading. *Cognitive Neuropsychology, 8,* 249–273.
Kay, J., & Hanley, J. R. (1999). Person-specific knowledge and knowledge of biological categories. *Cognitive Neuropsychology, 16,* 171–180.
Kay, J., Hanley, J. R., & Miles, R. (2001). Exploring the relationship between proper name anomia and word retrieval: A single case study. *Cortex, 37,* 501–517.
Kay, J., Lesser, R., & Coltheart, M. (1992). *PALPA: Psycholinguistic Assessments Of Language Processing in Aphasia.* Hove, UK: Lawrence Erlbaum Associates Ltd.
Kay, J., Lesser, R., & Coltheart, M. (1996). Clinical forum – Psycholinguistic Assessments Of Language Processing in Aphasia: An introduction. *Aphasiology, 10,* 159–180.
Kertesz, A. (1982). *Western Aphasia Battery.* New York: Grune & Stratton.
Kiran, S., Thompson, C. K., & Hashimoto, N. (2001). Training grapheme to phoneme conversion in patients with oral reading and naming deficits: A model-based approach. *Aphasiology, 15,* 855–876.
Lambon Ralph, M. A., Ellis, A. W., & Franklin, S. (1995). Semantic loss without surface dyslexia. *Neurocase, 1,* 363–369.
Lambon Ralph, M. A., Jarvis, C., & Ellis, A. W. (1997). Life in a mirrored world: Report of a case showing mirror reversal in reading and writing and for non-verbal materials. *Neurocase, 3,* 249–258.
Lambon Ralph, M. A., Sage, K., & Ellis, A. W. (1996). Word meaning blindness: A new form of acquired dyslexia. *Cognitive Neuropsychology, 13,* 617–639.
Law, S-P., & Orr, B. (2001). A case study of acquired dyslexia and dysgraphia in Chinese: Evidence for non-semantic pathways for reading and writing in Chinese. *Cognitive Neuropsychology, 18,* 729–748.

Maneta, A., Marshall, J., & Lindsay, J. (2001). Direct and indirect therapy for word and sound deafness. *International Journal of Language and Communication Disorders*, *36*, 91–106.

Marshall, J. (1996). The PALPA: A commentary and consideration of the clinical implications. *Aphasiology*, *10*, 197–202.

Marshall, J., Black, M., & Byng, S. (1999). *Working with sentences: A handbook for aphasia therapists* (pp. 1–41). London: Winslow Press.

Marshall, J., Pring, T., Chiat, S., & Robson, J. (2001). When ottoman is easier than chair: An inverse frequency effect in jargon aphasia. *Cortex*, *37*, 33–53.

Marslen-Wilson, W. D., & Tyler, L. K. (1997). Dissociating types of mental computation. *Nature*, *397*, 592–594.

Martin, A., & Caramazza, A. (2003). Neuropsychological and neuroimaging perspectives on conceptual knowledge: An introduction. *Cognitive Neuropsychology*, *20*(3/4/5/6), 195–212.

Morris, J., Franklin, S., Ellis, A. W., Turner, J. E., & Bailey, P. J. (1996). Remediating a speech perception deficit in an aphasic patient. *Aphasiology*, *10*, 137–158.

Morrison, C. M., & Ellis, A. W. (1995). The roles of word frequency and age of acquisition in word naming and lexical decision. *Journal of Experimental Psychology: Learning, Memory & Cognition*, *21*, 116–174.

Mummery, C. J., Ashburner, J., Scott, S. K., & Wise, R. J. S. (1999). Functional neuroimaging of speech perception in six normal and two aphasic subjects. *Journal of the Acoustical Society of America*, *106*, 449–457.

Nickels, L. (2002). Theoretical and methodological issues in the cognitive neuropsychology of spoken word production. *Aphasiology*, *16*, 3–19.

Nickels, L., & Cole-Virtue, J. (2004). Reading tasks from PALPA: How do controls perform on visual lexical decision, homophony, rhyme, and synonym judgements? *Aphasiology*, *18*, 103–126.

Nickels, L., & Howard, D. (1994). A frequent occurrence? Factors affecting the production of semantic errors in aphasic naming. *Cognitive Neuropsychology*, *11*, 289–320.

Ogden, J. A. (1996). Phonological dyslexia and phonological dysgraphia following left and right hemispherectomy. *Neuropsychologia*, *34*, 905–918.

Patterson, K., & Behrmann, M. (1997). Frequency and consistency effects in a pure surface dyslexic patient. *Journal of Experimental Psychology: Human Perception and Performance*, *23*, 1217–1231.

Patterson, K., & Hodges, J. R. (1992). Deterioration of word meaning: Implications for reading. *Neuropsychologia*, *30*, 1025–1040.

Patterson, K. E., & Marcel, A. (1992). Phonological ALEXIA or PHONOLOGICAL alexia. In J. Alegria, J. Holender, J. Junca de Morais, & M. Radeau (Eds.), *Analytic approaches to human cognition*. Elsevier Science Publishers.

Pedersen, P. M., Vinter, K., & Olsen, T. S. (2001). Improvement of oral naming by unsupervised computerised rehabilitation. *Aphasiology*, *15*, 151–169.

Reich, S., Chou, T-L., & Patterson, K. (2003). Acquired dysgraphia in Chinese: Further evidence on the links between phonology and orthography. *Aphasiology*, *17*, 585–604.

Reuter-Lorenz, P. A., & Brunn, J. L. (1990). A prelexical basis for letter-by-letter reading: A case study. *Cognitive Neuropsychology*, *7*, 1–20.

Riddoch, M. J., & Humphreys, G. W. (1993). *BORB: The Birmingham Object Recognition Battery*. Hove, UK: Lawrence Erlbaum Associates Ltd.

Scarna, A., & Ellis, A. W. (2002). On the assessment of grammatical gender knowledge in aphasia: The danger of relying on explicit, metalinguistic tasks. *Language and Cognitive Processes*, *17*, 185–201.

Schwartz, M. F., Saffran, E. M., & Marin, O. S. (1980). The word order problem in agrammatism: I. Comprehension. *Brain and Language*, *10*, 249–262.

Scott, S. S., Young, A. W., Calder, A. J., Hellawell, D. J., Aggleton, J. P., & Johnson, M. (1997). Impaired auditory recognition of fear and anger following bilateral amygdala lesions. *Nature*, *385*, 254–257.

Sieratzki, J. S., Calvert, G. A., Brammer, M., David, A., & Woll, B. (2001). Accessibility of spoken, written, and sign language in Landau-Kleffner syndrome: A linguistic and functional MRI study. *Epileptic Disorders*, *3*, 79–89.

Snodgrass, J., & Vanderwart, M. (1980). A standardised set of 260 pictures: Norms for name agreement, image agreement, familiarity and visual complexity. *Journal of Experimental Psychology: Human Learning and Memory*, *6*, 174–215.

Snowden, J. S., Griffiths, H. L., & Neary, D. (1996). Semantic–episodic memory interactions in semantic dementia: Implications for retrograde memory function. *Cognitive Neuropsychology*, *13*, 1101–1137.

Spencer, K. A., Doyle, P. J., McNeil, M. R., Wambaugh, J. L., Park, G., & Caroll, B. (2000). Examining the facilitative effects of rhyme in a patient with output lexicon damage. *Aphasiology*, *14*, 567–584.

Tree, J. J., Perfect, T. J., Hirsh, K. W., & Copstick, S. (2001). Deep dysphasic performance in non-fluent progressive aphasia: A case study. *Neurocase, 7*, 473–488.

Tyler, L. K., de Mornay Davies, P., Anokhina, R., Longworth, C., Randall, B., & Marslen-Wilson, W. D. (2002). Dissociations in processing past tense morphology: Neuropathology and behavioral studies. *Journal of Cognitive Neuroscience, 14*, 79–94.

Valle, F., & Cuetos, F. (1995). *EPLA: Evaluacion del procesamiento linguistico en la afasia.* Hove, UK: Lawrence Erlbaum Associates Ltd.

Varley, R., & Siegal, M. (2000). Evidence for cognition without grammar from causal reasoning and "theory of mind" in an agrammatic aphasic patient. *Current Biology, 10*, 723–726.

Weekes, B., & Chen, H-Q. (1999). Surface dyslexia in Chinese. *Neurocase, 5*, 161–172.

Weekes, B., Coltheart, M., & Gordon, E. (1997). Deep dyslexia and right hemisphere reading: A regional cerebral blood flow study. *Aphasiology, 11*, 1139–1158.

Weekes, B., Davies, R. A., Parris, B. A., & Robinson, G. (2003). The effects of age-of-acquisition and consistency on spelling in surface dysgraphia. *Aphasiology, 17*, 563–584.

Zeigler, J. C., Stone, G. O., & Jacobs, A. M. (1997). What is the pronunciation of –ough and the spelling for /u/? A database for computing feedforward and feedback consistency in English. *Behaviour Research Methods, Instruments and Computers, 29*, 600–618.

APHASIOLOGY, 2004, *18* (2), 153–179

# Why cabbage and not carrot?: An investigation of factors affecting performance on spoken word to picture matching

Jennifer Cole-Virtue and Lyndsey Nickels

*Macquarie University, Sydney, Australia*

*Background*: Word–picture matching tasks have been widely used to assess semantic processing in aphasia, but as yet have received little critical evaluation. Successful performance on a word–picture matching task employs several components of the language-processing system, including lexical and semantic processing of word stimuli and the visual and semantic processing of picture stimuli. Hence it is not only semantic impairments that can affect performance on this task—breakdown in processing at any point from early auditory or visual processing of the word or visual perception of the pictures can affect accuracy. Consequently, performance on a word–picture matching task might be affected by psycholinguistic variables that pertain to any of these levels of processing, such as imageability, word length, word frequency, and the relationship of the distractors to the target.

*Aims*: This study aimed to investigate the factors affecting word–picture matching performance, using one of the most widely used word–picture matching tasks (Subtest 47, Spoken word–picture matching, from PALPA; Kay, Lesser, & Coltheart, 1992).

*Methods and Procedures*: The performance and error patterns of 54 participants with aphasia and 51 elderly control participants, who had completed spoken word–picture matching (subtest number 47) from PALPA, were evaluated. Correlation and regression analyses were used to investigate effects of psycholinguistic variables on performance (frequency, imageability, number of phonemes, semantic and visual similarity, and word association).

*Outcomes and Results*: No variable was found to significantly affect control performance, due to ceiling effects. Imageability, semantic similarity, and word association affected the aphasic participant group performance. Six of the individuals with aphasia showed a significant effect on performance of at least one of four variables; imageability, semantic similarity, frequency, and word association.

*Conclusions*: This study demonstrates that three psycholinguistic variables significantly affect the performance of both the group with aphasia and some individual participants with aphasia. It suggests that accuracy can be influenced not only by the nature of the relationship of the stimuli within the test but also by the individual level of language processing breakdown. Clinicians and researchers need to be mindful of this when using word–picture matching as the basis of their assessment of semantic processing in aphasia.

Address correspondence to: Jennifer Cole-Virtue, Macquarie Centre for Cognitive Science (MACCS), Division of Linguistics & Psychology, Macquarie University, Sydney, NSW 2109, Australia. Email: jcole@maccs.mq.edu.au

Thanks to Janice Kay, Wendy Best, and the Prince of Wales and Prince Henry Hospitals' Speech Pathology Departments, Sydney, for their provision of and access to subject data. Thanks also to Max Coltheart and two anonymous reviewers for helpful comments on an earlier draft of this paper. Lyndsey Nickels was funded by an Australian Research Council QEII fellowship during the preparation of this paper.



http://www.tandf.co.uk/journals/pp/02687038.html DOI:10.1080/02687030344000517

In its evolution, the assessment of aphasia has seen many changes, none more provoking than the advent of cognitive neuropsychology. The objective of cognitive neuropsychology is to "provide formal characterisation of the mental structures and operations that subserve human cognitive capacity" (Caramazza, 1984, p. 384). Cognitive neuropsychological investigation of language ability has become a widely accepted approach to the assessment and treatment of the individual with aphasia. Assessment aims to identify which components of language processing are impaired and which are functioning relatively normally. Here we focus on the assessment of semantic processing abilities using word–picture matching tasks.

Word–picture matching is probably the most widely used method of investigating semantic processing. Word–picture matching is far from a new task, and appears in many "traditional" aphasia batteries (e.g., Boston Diagnostic Aphasia Examination, Goodglass & Kaplan, 1972; Western Aphasia Battery, Kertesz, 1982) and vocabulary tests (e.g., Peabody Picture Vocabulary Test, Dunn & Dunn, 1981). However, with the advent of cognitive neuropsychology there has been a proliferation of the use of these tasks while controlling more carefully for the type and nature of distractors as argued was vital by Bishop and Byng (1984).

Many earlier research papers used word–picture matching tests devised by the authors (e.g., Butterworth, Howard, & McLoughlin, 1984; Kay & Ellis, 1987; Miceli, Amitrano, Capasso, & Caramazza, 1996). However, more recently, word–picture matching assessments have become more widely available to clinicians and researchers (e.g., Test of lexical understanding with visual and semantic distractors—LUVS, Bishop & Byng, 1984; ADA comprehension battery, Franklin, Turner, & Ellis, 1992), especially following the publication of PALPA (Psycholinguistic Assessments of Language Processing in Aphasia, Kay, Lesser, & Coltheart, 1992). In order to determine whether poor performance on a word–picture matching task was due specifically to a semantic impairment, Bishop and Byng (1984) argue that it is essential to have both semantically related and unrelated distractors. Hence, the focus of this paper will be on tasks where a single word is presented and has to be matched to one of a choice of pictures, which (minimally) includes the target, a semantically related distractor, and an unrelated distractor. We also focus on spoken word–picture matching tasks where a heard word is to be matched, rather than the written equivalent of the task.

To complete a spoken word–picture matching task the subject must rely on particular components of the language-processing model (see Figure 1), specifically, auditory-lexical processing of words and the semantic processing of words and pictures. Butterworth et al. (1984) state, "in a pointing task, auditory input is used to access the lexical entry, which is then used to access a semantic representation and thereby gains access to a representation of the object/picture to be pointed to" (p. 421). In addition, the picture needs to be identified and its semantic representation accessed. Thus the completion of a spoken word–picture match task requires the processing of stored meanings from both lexical semantics (the spoken target word) and conceptual semantics (the stimulus pictures). The correct processing of this information will determine the subject's picture selection response. If, for example, the target item is "dog", the subject will be given the word "dog" and have a choice of pictures of a dog, a cat, and a tree. If there is no impairment, then the word and the picture of "dog" should activate features in the semantic system such as, "barks/has fur/domestic/four legs/tail"[1] and the convergence of

[1] We use a featural semantic representation purely as a means of illustrating the example and do not intend this to imply that this is necessarily an accurate reflection of how semantic representations are actually structured in the human language system.

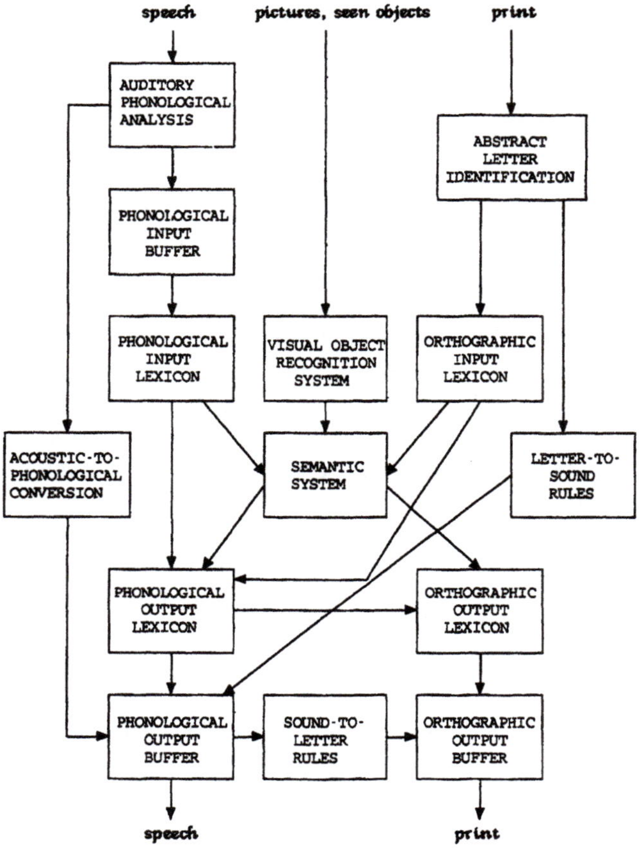


**Figure 1.** An information processing model of the lexicon (Kay et al., 1992).

this information should enable the correct identification of the target picture. However, if the semantic system is damaged, then on hearing ‘‘dog’’ a set of features may be activated that, for example, could be equally consistent with either DOG or CAT, such as ‘‘has fur/domestic/four legs/tail’’. In this case the incorrect choice of the close semantic distractor picture, cat, may be selected, resulting in a semantic error. Only in the case of severe semantic damage (where little or no semantic information is available) would the unrelated distractor, tree, be selected.

However, it is not only semantic impairments that can affect performance on word–picture matching—breakdown in processing at any point from early auditory processing of the word or visual perception of the pictures can also affect accuracy. Hence, subject performance on a word–picture matching task might be affected by psycholinguistic variables that affect any of these levels of processing including imageability, word length, word frequency, and the relationship of the semantic distractors to the target word (Bishop & Byng, 1984; Schuell, Jenkins, & Landis, 1961). Each of these variables will be discussed in relation to previously reported effects on comprehension for both normal and aphasic participant performance.

Imageability and/or concreteness are the variables whose effects on comprehension have been most widely investigated and reported. Imageability is a rated measure that refers to ‘‘normal subjects’ ratings of how easy it is to create a visual or auditory image of the referent corresponding to the word’’ (Coltheart, 1981). Like imageability, concreteness is a rated measure referring to how accessible to sensory experience normal subjects rate the referent of the word (Coltheart, 1981). Concreteness is highly correlated with imageability and the terms are often used interchangeably. The rated imageability of a word has been shown to affect the speed and/or accuracy of processing for both non-impaired participants and those with aphasia (and/or acquired dyslexia) and is generally considered to reflect semantic processing (Franklin, Howard, & Patterson, 1995). Effects of imageability/concreteness on comprehension tasks have been widely reported in cases of deep dyslexia (Coltheart, Patterson, & Marshall, 1980) and aphasia (Franklin, 1989; Franklin et al., 1995, Franklin, Turner, Lambon Ralph, Morris, & Bailey, 1996). Commonly, participants show poorer performance on comprehension tasks where the words are abstract/low imageability compared to words that are concrete/high imageability.

Franklin et al. (1995) in their study of DRB, a man with aphasia, found a strong effect of word imageability on his performance in all auditory word comprehension tasks. Franklin et al. (1996) considered that such reports are common in individuals with aphasia who have semantic or lexical deficits that are specific to auditory processing. They reported the case of Dr O whose comprehension of spoken words was affected by both imageability and word length. On a word definition task, Dr O showed improved performance as the imageability of the stimulus increased. If we consider that imageability/concreteness are semantic in nature, then by examining the effect of these variables on task performance we can obtain information regarding aspects of the semantic processing abilities of individual participants.

Word length has also been found to affect the performance of individuals with aphasia; it can be measured in terms of number of syllables and/or phonemes. Effects of number of phonemes on the performance of participants with aphasia have predominantly been reported in word production, usually with shorter words more accurately produced than longer words (Nickels & Howard, 1995; but see Best, 1995). However, word length has also been found to affect auditory comprehension in aphasia. Howard and Franklin (1988) presented the case of MK, who showed a reverse length effect on his ability to understand spoken words; that is, his comprehension was more accurate with longer words. Howard and Franklin suggest that MK finds short words more difficult as they are highly (phonologically) confusable because they have more neighbours than longer words (i.e., there are more words that differ by one phoneme from short words, e.g, cat, than from long words, e.g., caterpillar).

Word frequency has been recognised as an important factor in word recognition for participants with aphasia and refers to the "frequency of usage of a word in the language" (Schuell et al., 1961, p. 30). Word frequency is usually obtained by objective counts from large samples of spoken and/or written language (e.g., Baayen, Piepenbrock, & Van Rijn, 1993). Frequency effects are generally attributed to the ease of retrieval of the word form in the lexicon (e.g., Forster, 1990; Morton, 1970). High frequency words are retrieved faster and more accurately than low frequency words. Frequency effects have been examined in relation to the performance of aphasic individuals on spoken word–picture matching tasks. Butterworth et al. (1984) and Forde and Humphreys (1995) found no significant effects of word frequency on performance (see also Cipolotti & Warrington, 1995). However, Germani and Pierce (1995) examined semantic attribute knowledge using pointing tasks and found that word frequency had a significant role in the accuracy of attribute identification. They suggested that the comprehension of participants with aphasia was influenced by word frequency and that it might also affect the depth of their comprehension. Hence, while the role of frequency in the lexical process of spoken word recognition is well established (Schuell et al., 1961), the effects of word frequency on the semantic processing aspects of spoken word comprehension are not so clear.

In a word–picture matching task the frequency of both the target and the distractors needs to be considered when evaluating the effect that frequency may have on performance. If accurate comprehension is affected by frequency, one might expect that a low frequency target would generally be more error-prone than a high frequency target. However, consider the situation where a low frequency target (e.g., button) has a (close) semantic distractor that is even lower in frequency (e.g., zip). In this case, one might expect the target to be selected accurately, because despite being low frequency it is still relatively higher in frequency than the other response option. Similarly, a high frequency item (e.g., boy) may attract an error, if the distractor provided is of even higher frequency (e.g., girl). Hence, by this argument, it is not the absolute frequency of the target that is important but the relative frequency of target and distractor. In some studies the target and distractor are matched for frequency to specifically control for this factor. However, this has not been the case for all previous investigations and it may be the case that the equivocal findings in the past are a result of attention to target frequency only (see Butterworth et al., 1984).

As the discussion above makes clear, in addition to psycholinguistic properties of the targets, the relationship between the target and distractor items may also affect performance in word–picture matching. The nature of the relationship between the distractor and the target items can be further clarified by measures such as semantic similarly and word association ratings. Each of these measures will be discussed in turn.

Morris (1997) used ratings of semantic similarity between items in a spoken word–picture verification task. She used the concept of semantic relatedness to quantify the variability of the relationship between target and semantic distractors. Young non-aphasic participants were asked to rate how related pairs of category co-ordinates were in meaning. Morris (1997) reports that for some (but not all) of her participants with aphasia the semantic similarity ratings of target and distractor items affected performance on a spoken word–picture matching task. For these participants, performance was more accurate for items where the semantic relatedness rating between target and distractor was low (i.e., they were less similar). Performance deteriorated as the semantic relatedness rating of the target and distractor increased.

Measures of word association are obtained by asking participants to say or write the first word that comes to mind for each target word (Lesser, 1981). Word association is thought to reflect lexical-level relationships where words can be associated that would not normally be semantically linked, for instance, the words antique and vase have no semantic relationship (they are not from the same category for example) yet they are associated from their linguistic co-occurrence in the phrase "antique vase" (Coltheart, 1980), similarly for the example "blue moon".[2] Of course, there are also word pairs that bear both a lexical associative and a semantic relationship to the target (e.g., cup and saucer, which both occur in the same linguistic context and are from within the same category).

Both categorical and lexical-associative relationships have been examined in the semantic priming literature in reading aloud and lexical decision tasks (see Neely, 1991,

[2] Note, however, that semantic errors that are classified as associative in the aphasic spoken word production literature (e.g., grass–wind, saxophone–soul) are not necessarily *lexically* associated as measured by word association norms (Nickels, 1997). It would appear that there are two different ways that "associative" has been used in the classification of semantic errors: first those with a "lexical association" (as measured by the word association norms), Second, there are those semantic errors that occur in a similar semantic context (e.g., pen–desk).

for a review).[3] In many of these studies primes have been both semantically and associatively related to the targets, with the result that independent effects of semantic and associative relationships have been obscured. However, in a cued speeded word-reading task, Murphy (1999) found that non-aphasic participants did not differ in their reaction times to words that were associated and semantically related versus words that were purely semantically related, suggesting that associative relationships may not play an important role in speed of processing for lexical access. In contrast, McRae and Boisvert (1998) found that degree of featural (categorical) similarity between targets and primes is important in producing priming effects on lexical decision in non-aphasic participants. This supports Morris's (1997) finding and suggests that featural similarity of items (semantic similarity) may hinder the performance of some people with aphasia, but perhaps (lexical) associative relationships may not affect performance.

In summary the aim of this paper is to investigate the factors affecting word–picture matching performance in aphasia. Word–picture matching has been widely used as a tool to assess semantic processing, yet has received relatively little evaluation. We are specifically focusing on the Spoken word–picture matching subtest (no. 47) from PALPA (Psycholinguistic Assessments of Language Processing in Aphasia; Kay et al., 1992), as one of the most widely used published clinical and research materials for assessing semantic processing skills in people with aphasia. Hence we will investigate whether the nature of the relationship between target and close semantic distractor stimuli in PALPA subtest 47 and other psycholinguistic variables affects the performance of control participants and individuals with aphasia.

## METHOD

### Participants with aphasia

The participants in this study comprised 54 individuals with aphasia. The age range for the group was 18–90 years, with a mean age of 63.6 years (no age data were available for nine participants). Of these individuals 52 had suffered a unilateral left hemisphere cerebrovascular accident and 2 had received a head injury. Each participant had suffered only one vascular episode or only one instance of head trauma. A summary of the age and aetiology data for the participants with aphasia can be found in Appendix A. These individuals were relatively unselected except that they met the following criteria; there was no documented history of alcohol or drug abuse, psychiatric illness, dementia, or degenerative neurological condition, and English was their first language. They had a variety of aphasia types and time since onset of aphasia ranged from 4 weeks to more than 6 months. Of the participants in this study 21 had previously been involved in research in the UK and Australia, and the remaining 33 individuals were recruited from a local speech pathology department in Sydney. All participants had completed the PALPA spoken word–picture matching task (subtest 47).

### Control participants

The controls in this study comprised 31 British and 20 Australian neurologically intact individuals. These two groups were studied to establish whether there were any differ-

[3] Semantic priming refers to the fact that faster responses to word reading and lexical decision tasks have been found if subjects are shown a preceding word (a prime) that is semantically related to the target word.

ences in performance across the two cultural groups, and to provide a larger control group for analysis. The two groups were not matched in any way, except that both were intended as controls for the majority of participants with aphasia and hence comprised older individuals. The Australian participants had a mean age of 68.0 years (standard deviation: 3.86). Eight were male and twelve female. They were all elderly individuals, recruited from a local club for retired/semi-retired professional and business people. Many had received some level of tertiary education (mean years of education: 12.36 years, standard deviation: 1.86). None had a history of a vascular event and all had completed the PALPA spoken word–picture matching task (subtest 47). The data for the British control participants were taken from pre-publication testing carried out by the authors of PALPA (Kay, personal communication). These 31 control participants were partners of the individuals with aphasia who participated in the development of PALPA and on whom the authors based their descriptive statistics for this subtest (age: mean = 64.6, standard deviation = 12.46; years of education: mean = 9.34, standard deviation: 0.91; 22 male, 9 female).

## Description of PALPA subtest 47

The participant is required to listen to a spoken word and then select the correct picture from a choice of the target and four distractor pictures. Kay et al. (1992) state that the distractor pictures have specific relationships to the target word. There are 40 target items and the distractor pictures for each target consist of "a close semantic distractor from the same superordinate category, a more distant semantic distractor, a visually similar distractor and an unrelated distractor" (Kay et al., 1992, subtest 47, p. 1). For example, for the target word "carrot" the distractor pictures are "cabbage" (close semantic), "lemon" (distant semantic), "saw" (visually related), and "chisel" (unrelated) (see Figure 2). The unrelated and visually related distractors are related to each other semantically but not to the target item. This control feature has been incorporated to prevent the subject responding on the basis of perceived semantic category.

## Psycholinguistic variables

Control participant and aphasic participant performance was examined using seven psycholinguistic measures; imageability, number of phonemes (word length), target log frequency, target-close distractor frequency difference, semantic similarity, visual similarity, and word association.

*Imageability (Imag).* Imageability ratings for 27 of the target items were taken from the MRC database (Coltheart, 1981). A further eight imageability ratings were taken from a set of object name norms (Morrison, Chappell, & Ellis, 1997). The Morrison et al. set of imageability ratings were linearly transformed so that they could be used in conjunction with those from the MRC databse, using the same method as for the merging of ratings from different sets of data in the MRC database (MRC Psycholinguistic Database User Manual: Version 1; Coltheart, 1981).

*Log frequency (LF).* Spoken word frequency counts were taken from the Celex database (Baayen et al., 1993) and log transformed.

*Target-close distractor frequency difference (T/CSD Freq diff).* The log frequency value for the target and the close semantic distractor were separately calculated from their

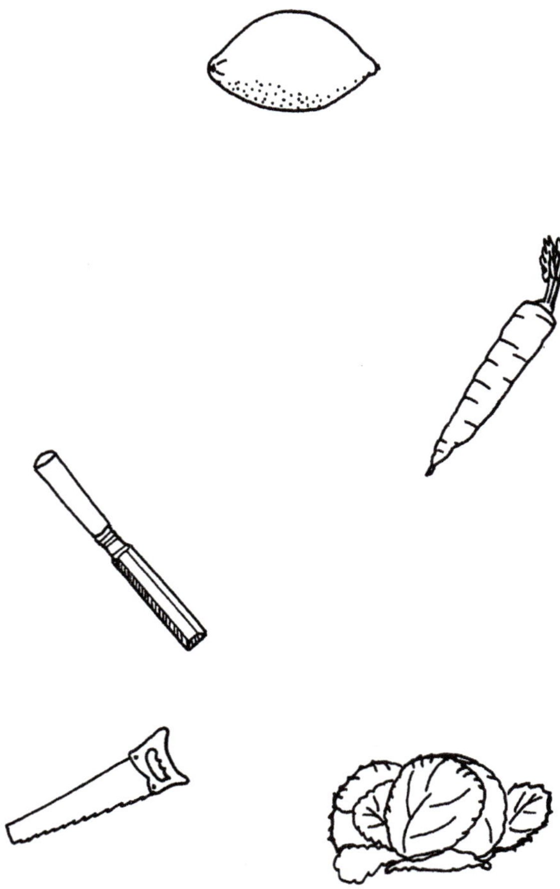

**Figure 2.** PALPA subtest 47, item 1.

Celex frequency values. The target-close distractor frequency difference was the difference between the log frequency value for the target and the log frequency value for the close semantic distractor.

*Semantic similarity (Semsim) and visual similarity (Vissim).* Ratings of semantic similarity and visual similarity were collected from 20 Australian non-aphasic participants, who were undergraduate psychology students and participated in the experiment as part of the fulfilment of their course requirements. The participants were asked to judge how semantically related/similar and visually related/similar the close semantic distractor, distant semantic distractor, and unrelated distractor were to their corresponding target item. Participants were asked to use a rating scale of 1–7 to reflect whether words were highly unrelated, moderately related, or highly related. Only the ratings of similarity between the targets and their close semantic distractors have been used to evaluate participant performance.

*Word association (Assoc).* To obtain a measure of the degree of association between the 40 targets and their close semantic distractors in subtest 47, the Edinburgh Association Norms were used (CSID, 1996). The measure of association used is the percentage of participants who produced a particular response to a target. A high percentage response indicates a high degree of association. Five of the forty targets (12.5%; hosepipe, lobster, paintbrush, stirrup, underpants) were not found in the EAN and therefore could not be included in the analyses.

## Statistical methodology

Due to intercorrelations between the variables (see Appendix B) it is impossible to distinguish effects of different variables on performance using correlation analysis. Therefore regression analyses are performed in order to identify the unique effects of each variable once the effects of intercorrelations between variables have been accounted for. Although the correlation data for group and individual performance will be presented, primarily the regression data will be discussed. All regression data use a reduced set of stimuli ($n$ = 35) due to the missing values for the word association variable (excluded targets: hosepipe, lobster, paintbrush, stirrup, underpants).

It is important to note that as the number of stimuli in the analyses is relatively small ($n$ = 35), there are two possible problems with the individual analyses presented here. First, the reliability of the analysis can be doubtful, particularly for those individuals who make small numbers of errors. However, countering this is the fact that the power of the analysis is relatively limited, hence the chances of a variable reaching significance are relatively small. Because of the concern regarding reliability, we have been relatively conservative in our discussions of the individual results and only discuss the results when a variable shows a consistently significant effect across both correlation and regression.

Group analyses: Below are the details of each analysis and the variables whose effects on both control and aphasic group performance will be examined.

*Analysis 1 & 2.* Correlation & multiple regression with log frequency, imageability, number of phonemes, semantic similarity, visual similarity, T/CSD frequency difference, word association.

*Analysis 3.* Multiple regression with log frequency, imageability, number of phonemes, semantic similarity, word assocociation. VIsual similarity was excluded from this analysis as it correlates highly with semantic similarity and hence the chances of either variable reaching significance are reduced. Similarly, log frequency and T/CSD frequency difference are highly correlated hence only one measure of frequency (log frequency) was included in this reduced analysis.

# RESULTS

## Control group analyses

The accuracy for both control groups is shown in Table 1. Eighteen of the British control group participants did not make any errors and the remaining thirteen participants made a total of 21 errors on ten targets. Only five participants made more than two errors. Eleven of the Australian control group participants did not make any errors and the remaining nine participants made twelve errors (range of 1–3 errors per participant) on seven targets. Eleven of these errors were spontaneously self-corrected.

There was no significant difference between the control groups for mean score or mean error rates. An unrelated $t$-test to examine if there was a difference in overall accuracy between the groups was non-significant ($t$ = 0.201, df 50, $p$ = .8412), as was a related $t$-test examining performance on items across both groups ($t$ = 0.076, df 39, $p$ =

TABLE 1
Mean scores for the control and aphasic groups

| *Participant group* | *Mean score* | *Standard deviation* | *Score for two standard deviations** | *Number of participants > 2 SD* |
|---|---|---|---|---|
| British control ($n$ = 31) | 39.3 | 1.07 | 37.20 | 1 |
| Australian control ($n$ = 20) | 39.4 | 0.82 | 37.70 | 1 |
| Total control ($n$ = 51) | 39.37 | 0.97 | 37.42 | |
| Aphasic ($n$ = 54) | 30.63 | 7.52 | 15.59 | 2 |

* This column represents the lower limit of accuracy required to be within two standard deviations of the mean for that group of participants.

.9400). Thus data from the two groups will be combined henceforth. Item accuracy for the combined control groups ranged from 88–100%. Both control groups made predominantly close semantic distractor errors. See Appendix C for a listing of the errors made by the control groups. As performance was so close to ceiling (mean error per item = 0.6) no significant effects were found in the multiple regression or correlation analyses (see Table 2).

## Aphasic group analyses

As shown in Table 1 (earlier) the mean score for the aphasic participant group for the 40 test items was 30.63 (standard deviation 7.52). Two participants scored more than two standard deviations below the mean. All participants made errors, ranging from 1–34 errors per participant. The predominant error type was the close semantic distractor (13% of responses, 57% of errors). This pattern is similar to that of the combined control groups (2% of responses, 64% of errors were close semantic distractor errors).

In analysis 1 (Table 3) the aphasic group accuracy correlated significantly with semantic similarity, visual similarity, and word association. In a multiple regression incorporating the same variables (analysis 2) none of the variables reached significance.

TABLE 2
Control group analyses

| | | | *LF* | *Phon* | *Semsim* | *Vissim* | *T/CSD Freq diff* | *Assoc* | *Imag* |
|---|---|---|---|---|---|---|---|---|---|
| | | *N* | *40* | *40* | *40* | *40* | *40* | *35* | *35* |
| Analysis 1 | Correlations | $r$ | 0.24 | −0.251 | −0.121 | −0.194 | 0.101 | 0.289 | 0.055 |
| | | $p$ | ns | ns | ns | ns | ns | ns | ns |
| Analysis 2 | Multiple regression | $t$ | −0.252 | −1.57 | 0.217 | −0.941 | 0.939 | 1.386 | 1.665 |
| | | $p$ | ns | ns | ns | ns | ns | ns | ns |
| Analysis 3 | Multiple regression | $t$ | 0.722 | −1.986 | −0.742 | – | – | 1.407 | 1.515 |
| | | $p$ | ns | ns | ns | | | ns | ns |

LF: log frequency; Phon: number of phonemes; Semsim: semantic similarity rating between target and close semantic distractor; Vissim: visual similarity rating between target and close semantic distractor; T/CSD Freq diff: the difference between the target and close semantic distractor frequency; Assoc: word association; Imag: rated imageability; ns: non significant, $p > .05$.

TABLE 3
Aphasic group analyses

| | | | *LF* | *Phon* | *Semsim* | *Vissim* | *T/CSD Freq diff* | *Assoc* | *Imag* |
|---|---|---|---|---|---|---|---|---|---|
| | | *N* | *40* | *40* | *40* | *40* | *40* | *35* | *35* |
| Analysis 1 | Correlations | *r* | −0.003 | −0.026 | −0.36 | −0.324 | −0.286 | 0.346 | 0.107 |
| | | *p* | ns | ns | 0.022 | 0.041 | ns | 0.042 | ns |
| Analysis 2 | Multiple regression | *t* | −1.178 | 0.759 | −1.474 | −0.788 | −0.24 | 1.894 | 2.03 |
| | | *p* | ns | ns | ns | ns | ns | ns | ns |
| Analysis 3 | Multiple regression | *t* | −1.779 | 0.837 | −2.782 | – | – | 2.404 | 2.237 |
| | | *p* | ns | ns | 0.010 | | | 0.023 | 0.034 |

LF: log frequency; Phon: number of phonemes; Semsim: semantic similarity rating between target and close semantic distractor; Vissim: visual similarity rating between target and close semantic distractor; T/CSD Freq diff: the difference between the target and close semantic distractor frequency; Assoc: word association; Imag: rated imageability; ns: non significant, $p > .05$.

In a further regression with a reduced set of variables (analysis 3), semantic similarity, imageability, and word association reached significance, all of which significantly affect aphasic performance.[4]

Although the control group was too near ceiling to show any significant effects on accuracy, there was a significant correlation ($r = .379, p = .016$) between the aphasic and control performance for mean number of errors per item. Hence, it seems likely that similar factors do affect performance for both groups.

## Analyses of individual performance for participants with aphasia

Appendix D presents the correlation results for those aphasic individuals who have effects at or approaching significance; regression results are only reported for those individuals with significant effects (see Table 4).

*Analysis 1: Correlation.* In analysis 1, the performance of two participants was significantly correlated with log frequency (SG negatively and LMT a positive correlation). Four participants were significantly and positively correlated with imageability (SW, PD, CB, RA). Eight participants were significantly correlated with number of phonemes, five positively (JO, LM, DO, AE, SG) and three negatively (HC, BMcB, SP). Four participants showed significant correlations with semantic similarity (JG, JO, WB, HC), HC showed a significant negative correlation. Five participants (WB, AE, CO, FrS) were significantly negatively correlated with visual similarity. The performance of two participants (BB, EM) was significantly negatively correlated with T/CSD frequency difference. One participant showed a significant positive correlation with word association (BR).

[4] The analyses were repeated including only those individuals with aphasia who performed outside normal limits on the assessment (seven individuals excluded using the criterion of 2 SD from the mean as recommended by Kay et al.). The results of the analyses using this revised group of participants were unchanged with the same variables reaching significance.

**TABLE 4**

**Individual participants with aphasia showing significant effects in logistic regression (5 and 7 variable analysis)**

| | *Accuracy* | | | *Analysis 2 (n = 35)* | | | | | | | *Analysis 3 (n = 35)* | | | | |
|---|---|---|---|---|---|---|---|---|---|---|---|---|---|---|---|
| *Subject* | *n* = 40 | *n* = 35 | *Logistic regression* | *LF* | *Imag* | *Phon* | *Sem Sim* | *Vis Sim* | *T/CSD Freq Diff* | *Assoc* | *LF* | *Imag* | *Phon* | *Sem Sim* | *Assoc* |
| HE | 23 | 22 | Full Wald | 0.250 | 3.989 | 1.649 | 0.123 | 0.078 | 0.083 | 0.031 | 0.845 | 4.174 | 1.793 | 0.554 | 0.114 |
| | | | p | 0.617 | **0.046** | 0.199 | 0.726 | 0.780 | 0.773 | 0.859 | 0.358 | **0.041** | 0.181 | 0.457 | 0.735 |
| JG | 31 | 29 | Full Wald | 0.000 | 0.000 | 0.000 | 0.000 | 0.000 | 0.000 | 0.000 | 0.027 | 0.015 | 0.005 | 4.930 | 2.074 |
| | | | p | 0.993 | 0.998 | 0.997 | 0.992 | 0.998 | 0.994 | 0.997 | 0.870 | 0.904 | 0.944 | **0.026** | 0.150 |
| JO | 35 | 30 | Full Wald | 0.000 | 0.001 | 0.000 | 0.001 | 0.001 | 0.001 | 0.000 | 0.413 | 1.414 | 1.356 | 4.122 | 0.102 |
| | | | p | 0.983 | 0.979 | 0.984 | 0.974 | 0.976 | 0.979 | 0.990 | 0.521 | 0.234 | 0.244 | **0.042** | 0.750 |
| SG | 23 | 23 | Full Ward | 3.572 | 0.146 | 3.368 | 0.428 | 0.146 | 0.185 | 3.390 | 4.800 | 0.173 | 3.419 | 0.287 | 3.875 |
| | | | p | 0.059 | 0.703 | 0.066 | 0.513 | 0.702 | 0.667 | 0.066 | **0.028** | 0.677 | 0.064 | 0.592 | **0.049** |
| JuG | 18 | 18 | Full Wald | 5.418 | 1.566 | 4.845 | 4.757 | 2.899 | 2.762 | 3.691 | 5.006 | 0.310 | 3.201 | 3.910 | 3.096 |
| | | | p | **0.020** | 0.211 | **0.028** | **0.029** | 0.089 | 0.097 | 0.055 | **0.025** | 0.578 | 0.074 | **0.048** | 0.078 |
| BR | 26 | 23 | Full Wald | 1.098 | 2.306 | 0.180 | 1.754 | 0.065 | 0.202 | 3.822 | 1.124 | 2.164 | 0.292 | 3.043 | 4.665 |
| | | | p | 0.295 | 0.129 | 0.671 | 0.185 | 0.799 | 0.653 | 0.051 | 0.289 | 0.141 | 0.589 | 0.081 | **0.031** |

Full Wald: All variables in the regression

(shaded) *p* = <.10

(boxed) *p* = <.05.

LF: Log Frequency; Imag: Imageability; Phon: number of Phonemes; Sem Sim: Semantic Similarity; Vis Sim: VIsual Similarity; T/CSD Freq Diff: T/CSD Frequency Difference; Assoc: Word Association.

*Analyses 2 & 3: Logistic regression.* A number of participants continued to show significant effects when intercorrelations between the variables had been accounted for using logistic regression. In analysis 2 (seven variables), participant HE showed a significant effect of imageability. One participant, JuG, showed a significant effect of log frequency, number of phonemes and a significant effect of semantic similarity. None of the participants showed an effect of visual similarity, T/CSD frequency difference or word association on their performance.

Analysis 3 was run with the reduced set of five variables. The following participants showed significant effects in the initial regression model; SG and JuG for log frequency, HE for imageability, JG, JO, and JuG for semantic similarity, and SG and BR for word association. No participants showed significant effects for number of phonemes.

## DISCUSSION

We are addressing the question ''Does the nature of the relationship between target and distractor stimuli in spoken word–picture matching (PALPA subtest 47) and other psycholinguistic variables affect the performance of control participants and individuals with aphasia?'' We examined the performance of non-aphasic participants and participants with aphasia (both as a group and individually) using both correlation and regression analyses. As there are only a small number of items in this subtest and hence a restricted number of participant errors to analyse, we are aware that there is a danger of the results being unreliable (see below for further discussion). As a result of these limitations, only consistent and robust effects on individual participant performance will be discussed.

The effects on performance of seven psycholinguistic variables were examined; rated imageability, rated semantic similarity, rated visual similarity, number of phonemes, log frequency, the frequency difference between the target and close semantic distractor, and the degree of word association between the target and close semantic distractor. None of these variables showed significant effects on accuracy for the control group. This is not surprising as the mean number of errors per item was very low, with many of the control participants scoring at ceiling. Nevertheless, it is of note that the Australian and British controls did not perform significantly differently on this assessment, suggesting that this British test is equally valid in the Australian context.[5] Control performance was found to correlate significantly with the performance of the group of participants with aphasia, suggesting that similar factors affected both groups.

Three variables significantly affected the aphasic group: semantic similarity, imageability, and word association. Each of these three variables also significantly affected the performance of at least one individual with aphasia. Additionally, two individuals with aphasia showed a significant effect of spoken word frequency on performance. In total, six of the participants with aphasia showed significant effects of at least one variable. Hence, despite the limitations resulting from a small number of items in the test itself and a restricted number of errors per participants to analyse, significant effects have been demonstrated to affect spoken word–picture matching performance for both the aphasic group and individuals with aphasia. We will discuss each of the variables in turn.

[5] However, the Australian controls used in this study as monolingual English speakers are only representative of a subset of the multicultural Australian population, hence broad applicability cannot be taken for granted.

## Imageability

Imageability was found to affect the performance of the aphasic group and of one individual participant, HE. Both the group and HE showed improved performance on higher imageability target items and were less accurate on target items of a lower imageability rating. These findings are consistent with previous reports of imageability effects on the performance of auditory comprehension tasks (Franklin, 1989; Franklin et al., 1996). However, these reports of imageability effects have usually been in tasks where stimuli have had a wider range of imageability values (including "abstract" words) and were not pictured or exclusively "concrete" items. Stimuli in spoken word–picture matching tasks are inevitably highly imageable, as they must be picturable items. Thus the range of imageability values is necessarily restricted and it is therefore surprising to find a significant effect of imageability on comprehension performance in this type of task. However, effects of imageability have been found in tasks involving exclusively picture stimuli. For example, Nickels and Howard (1995) found imageability effects on a picture–naming task for some individuals with aphasia. Why should it be that we see effects of imageability? Why is it that lower imageability words may be more susceptible to error in an impaired processing system?

Plaut and Shallice (1993) present a connectionist model of reading and suggest that concrete words have more semantic features and are represented more widely within the semantic system than abstract words. If lower imageability words have fewer features then it is feasible that in a damaged semantic system they may be more difficult to retrieve. In other words, items with high imageability ratings may be less susceptible to the effects of damage (e.g., in the form of noise) within the semantic system.

Several authors consider that imageability reflects the processing of meaning or semantic information both in comprehension and production (Franklin, 1989; Nickels & Howard, 1995). If we accept that effects of imageability reflect semantic processing (either in representation of semantic information or of access to those representations) then it is reasonable to surmise that for HE, who showed significant effects of imageability on spoken word–picture matching, a significant component of his aphasia is semantically based. Even though there is a significant diversity in the nature of the aphasia across the group, imageability also affects their performance on this task. These findings suggest that a semantic deficit is a likely source of the errors on this task, for at the very least, a substantial subset of the individuals within the group.

## Semantic similarity

The rated semantic similarity between the target and the close semantic distractor affected the performance of the aphasic participant group and three individual participants, JuG, JG, and JO. Both the group and the individual participants showed improved performance as the rated semantic similarity between the target and the close distractor decreased. This is to say, they were less accurate on items where the close semantic distractor was rated as highly semantically similar to the target word.

Before we go on to discuss why semantic similarity might affect performance, we must first reflect on the fact that semantic and visual similarity ratings as highly correlated (things that are semantically related often look alike, e.g., cat & dog, bowl & cup). We only ever found significant effects of semantic similarity in regression analyses where visual similarity was excluded (analysis 3). Hence, can we be sure that we have a "true" effect of semantic similarity? Four sources of evidence support the conclusion that the effect reflects semantic and not visual similarity. First, the fact that none of the individuals who showed significant effects of semantic similarity showed significant correlations with visual similarity, and for the group the correlation with semantic similarity was stronger than for visual similarity. Second, no individual showed a significant effect of visual similarity in analysis 2 (with both semantic and visual similarity in the analysis) but one, JuG, showed a significant effect of semantic similarity. Third, when we repeated analysis 3, replacing semantic similarity with visual similarity (and including the other four variables), unlike semantic similarity, visual similarity did not have a significant effect on performance for either JG (Wald = 2.254, $p$ = .133) or JO (Wald = 0.595, $p$ = .440). Finally, in a multiple regression with the three variables that significantly affect group performance (semantic similarity, imageability, and association) and visual similarity, visual similarity did not reach significance ($t$ = 0.780, $p$ = .442) for the group.

The finding of a significant effect of semantic similarity is consistent with Morris (1997) who found that the semantic similarity of the target and distractor affected performance in a spoken word–picture verification task. Morris found that the performance of participant JAC was affected by the semantic relatedness of the target and foil pairs. Like the participants reported here, JAC showed improved performance for pairs that had a low semantic relatedness rating.

So why might degree of semantic similarity affect the comprehension performance of participants with aphasia? Morris (1997) suggests that examining the number of shared semantic features between items may provide an "objective measure" of semantic similarity, and further, that this kind of featural analysis may be the basis of the semantic relatedness judgement when participants rate items. If we compare two pairs of items from subtest 47, "parachute-balloon" (semantic similarity rating of 4.5) and "comb–brush" (semantic similarity rating of 6.8) it is possible to explain why semantic similarity as a measure of featural overlap might affect accuracy. The pair "parachute" (which might have features such as: made of fabric/opens/aids descent/means of suspension in the air) and "balloon" (made of rubber/inflates/rises up/means of suspension in the air) share being a means of suspension in the air but otherwise have few features in common. There is less featural overlap and more to distinguish the items from each other. In contrast "comb" (with hypothetical features: teeth/hand held/for hair care) and "brush" (bristles/hand held/for hair care) seem to have more in common. If semantic processing is impaired and semantic information is compromised (whether through loss of or access to featural information) then those items that have less featural overlap are more likely to be distinguished from each other rather than those that share many things in common.

However, this "feature-based" explanation of semantic similarity may be simplistic. While it has been established that the semantic relatedness of a target and a distractor affects performance, adequately defining the properties of this type of relationship is not clear-cut. It would appear that factors affecting the rating of semantic relatedness could depend on the item being rated. Morris (1997) suggests that the features considered in this type of judgement may vary. For example, artefacts may be judged on their features of function or association, whereas for animals the judgement may be based on visual or perceptual features.

In PALPA subtest 47 the definition of a close semantic distractor by the authors is that it comes from the same superordinate category as the target. We would expect that those items sharing a superordinate category would have many semantic features in common. However, nine of the targets and their close semantic distractors are, in fact, judged to be semantic associates[6] and not co-ordinates from the same superordinate category. If number of shared features were a reflection of semantic relatedness it would be reasonable to expect that those targets and distractor items that share a superordinate would be rated as more highly semantically related than the item pairs that are semantically associated. However, although in the predicted direction, there were no significant difference between the mean semantic similarity for the target and distractor pairs that share superordinate category and for those that are semantically associated (co-ordinate pairs: mean 5.35, *SD* 0.88; semantic associate pairs: mean 4.95, *SD* 0.79; $t = 1.236$, df 38, $p = .112$, one-tailed). Clearly, semantic similarity is a broad concept and requires further definition. Although featural similarity is a consideration in semantic similarity ratings, the raters are also using other aspects of semantic knowledge about the context and association that items share. In other words it is not just featural similarity that is reflected in this measure.

Evidence from this study and Morris (1997) suggests that a semantic similarity measure is able to elucidate aspects of impaired semantic processing in auditory comprehension tasks for individuals with aphasia. This has implications for the assessment and treatment of this population. The design of materials for assessment and treatment of comprehension needs to be evaluated closely, and semantic similarity taken into account and controlled for in these tasks. It may also prove to be a useful factor to manipulate in the design of treatment studies for those participants who have semantically based comprehension deficits.

## Frequency

The log frequency of the target items in PALPA subtest 47 significantly affected the performance of two participants, JuG and SG, but did not significantly affect performance of the aphasic group overall. It might be predicted that participants should improve their performance as the frequency of the target increases, as these words have a higher level of resting activation and hence reach threshold more easily (Morton, 1970). However, for both JuG and SG, performance improved as the frequency of the target items decreased. In other words they were more accurate on low frequency target items.

It is also of interest that, despite the prediction in the introduction that it should be the relative frequency of target and distractor that is relevant rather than absolute frequency, there is no evidence that this was the case. Only two participants showed a significant correlation with T/CSD difference and this was not in the predicted direction (a significant negative correlation)—they showed more accurate performance when the T/CSD difference was smaller; in other words when the distractor was higher-frequency than the target, they were more accurate. There was no significant correlation with group performance and no individuals continued to show significant effects in the regression analysis.

How might we account for the reverse frequency effect? One possibility is that it could be a confound with word length and number of phonological neighbours. Low frequency words tend to be longer and are therefore more phonologically distinct (have few

[6] Target and close semantic distractor pairs were to be judged as either co-ordinates (from the same superordinate category) or semantic associates (items that go together in the world but that are NOT from the same superordinate category) See Cole-Virtue and Nickels (2004 this issue) for further discussion of this issue and critique of the subtest.

phonological neighbours) and as a result they are less confusable with other words. However, as number of phonemes was included in the analysis, this intercorrelation could not be a source of the effect. (In addition neither participant showed the predicted significant negative correlation between number of phonemes and accuracy.) Furthermore, when analysis 3 was repeated with the addition of the variable number of neighbours neither SG nor JuG showed an effect of neighbours on performance, but both continued to show a significant reverse effect of frequency. This would suggest that the reverse frequency effects are not due to any influence of phonological neighbours.

Another possible explanation for this reverse frequency effect may be the influence of other confounding variables that have not been considered in the analyses. One such variable is familiarity, which is correlated with log frequency. Familiarity is a measure where participants must rate how often they see, hear, or use that word (Gilhooly & Logie, 1980). Words that have a low familiarity rating also tend to be of a lower frequency. Nickels and Howard (1995) suggest that familiarity may be a more reliable measure of subjective frequency for lower frequency items. If it were the case that the reverse frequency effect is due to the unreliable nature of frequency counts for lower frequency items, then we might expect that any effect of familiarity would not be in the reverse direction. However, SG's performance was significantly negatively correlated with familiarity ($r = -0.420$, $p = .023$) and if log frequency is replaced by familiarity in the logistic regression analysis there is a trend to a reverse effect of familiarity ($B = -.016$, Wald $= 2.861$, $p = .091$). This suggests that SG is more accurate on targets with a lower familiarity rating and that the reverse direction of the frequency effect, for SG, may not be just an artefact of the unreliable frequency counts for the lower frequency items. However, JuG showed no sign of significant effects of familiarity (in correlation or regression analyses) and hence it is possible that the reverse frequency effect on her performance may be due to the unreliable nature of the frequency counts.

How can the reverse direction of the frequency effect be explained? Marshall, Pring, Chiat, and Robson (2001) present data from an aphasic participant who shows a reverse frequency effect in word production (picture naming) and suggest that interpretation of this effect poses a problem for current theories. Certainly it challenges the fact that in the unimpaired language system high frequency words are favoured over their low frequency counterparts (e.g., Morton, 1970). Marshall et al. propose that the reverse frequency effect could arise at the level of semantic processing, and explore the idea that for their participant, JP, the low frequency items have semantic properties that in some way facilitate the naming process. They suggest that lower frequency items may be more semantically distinct and share fewer features in common than items with a higher frequency. Thus, a high frequency item like "dog" would have competitors that share many features, such as "cat". These competitors would also be highly activated and might affect production of the target "dog". In comparison a lower frequency word, with fewer competitors that share features, would have less competition and result in a relative advantage for that target. However, rather than it being the number of *shared* features, it may be the number of *distinctive* (NON-shared) features that accounts for the advantage for lower frequency items. For example, "cat" (meows/has fur/pet/four legs/tail), "dog" (barks/has fur/pet/four legs/tail), "kangaroo" (tuts/has fur/wild/four legs/tail), and "beetle" (clicks/has shell/pet/six legs/wings) share features in common. Both "cat" and "dog" share the same four (has fur/pet/four legs/tail), "kangaroo" shares three (fur/four legs/tail) of these and "beetle" shares only one (pet). The remaining features for each item are such that "cat" and "dog" have one distinguishing feature (meow/barks respectively), "kangaroo" has two (tuts/wild). However, "beetle" has four distinguishing features that set it apart from the other items (clicks/wings/has shell/six legs). In the damaged semantic system, it may be the semantic information that distinguishes these items from each other rather than the shared or common features that facilitate item selection in a comprehension task. Such an explanation could account for participant SG's tendency to respond more accurately to lower frequency items in this word–picture matching task.[7] This is similar in essence to the account of semantics proposed by Plaut and Shallice (1993) in their distributed connectionist model of reading. In this theory concrete words are represented by more semantic features and have great featural overlap than abstract words. When their computational model is "lesioned", it is generally the higher-imageability words that are more accurate, as they have a greater number of features and are therefore less susceptible to damage (or noise) within the system. However, included in the model are semantic "clean-up" units which help the model settle into a stable pattern of activation corresponding to known concepts. As concrete words have greater overlap between their semantic features than abstract words, there is a greater reliance on the "clean-up" units for the concrete items. It follows then that when these units are "lesioned", it is the abstract words that are relatively less impaired compared to the concrete words. The parallels with the account discussed above are clear—the advantage for abstract words is due to the representations of abstract words having less featural overlap compared to concrete items. It is possible that the same might hold for low frequency words.

The accounts of reverse imageability and frequency effects have all hypothesised that these effects are a product of damaged semantic systems (see also Breedin, Saffran, & Coslett, 1994). In these instances the accessibility or loss of semantic information advantages items with less featural overlap and results in easier selection of these items, as within a damaged system they are more semantically distinct. It would seem to be a reasonable assumption that the reverse frequency effect seen for participant SG could be the result of faulty semantic processing rather than being purely lexically based. Certainly participant SG shows considerable semantic impairment (17 errors on subtest 47) which suggests that a semantic explanation could account for this reverse effect.

Reverse frequency effects on performance are not reported very often but they may contribute to the furthering of knowledge not only about the architecture of the semantic system but also about how semantic processing functions.

## Word association

Word association affected the aphasic group performance and the performance of participants SG and BR, individually. Both the group and the individual participants showed an unpredicted effect: accuracy improved as the rated association of the target and distractor item increased. These results suggests that there is a facilitatory effect on this semantic processing task for items that have an associative relationship. This is in contrast to the results for the group and individual performance in terms of semantic similarity, where accuracy increased as the semantic similarity between items decreased. The differing directions of these effects suggest that within this task semantic similarity and word association may reflect different levels of processing, semantic and lexical

[7] Of course, the empirical question is whether words that are less frequent do indeed have more distinguishing semantic features. Although beyond the scope of this study, this is an important area for future research.

respectively. Alternatively, they may reflect different processing within the semantic system for featural and associative relationships. The complexity of a task involving the matching of words and pictures makes more detailed conclusions difficult without further experimental exploration. Although the effect of word association relationships is discussed in the priming literature (see Neely, 1991, for a review) it has not been addressed within the context of this type of task. Moreover, in this literature, both associative and categorical relationships are argued (if anything) to speed processing in lexical decision and word reading, and the two have not been distinguished in categorisation tasks.

## Effects of number of phonemes

In this study the number of phonemes in the target words did not independently contribute to performance for either the group or the individuals with aphasia. Hence, for this semantic task we have no evidence for word length contributing to accuracy.

## Reliability

Before we conclude we should like to briefly discuss further some issues regarding reliability. We have noted that because of the small number of items in the test ($n = 40$; and an even smaller number in our analyses ($n = 35$) the reliability of our results is likely to be restricted. This is particularly true for a comprehension test where there is an element of chance (unlike picture naming, for example). Hence for some individuals some items may be correct by chance, inflating their accuracy. However, the small number of items means that the power of the analysis is relatively limited, hence the chances of a variable reaching significance are relatively small. Thus we should like to stress that even if a variable fails to reach significance for an individual on this assessment, it does not mean that they might not show a significant effect with a larger sample (see also Cole-Virtue & Nickels, 2004 this issue).

Finally, a clinically important point to note is that the relatively small number of items also means that the assessment lacks sensitivity to discriminate between degrees of semantic impairment. This is especially true for those individuals with mild–moderate semantic impairments. Furthermore, some of those individuals who score within the range of controls on this assessment may be revealed to have semantic impairments when assessed using ‘‘harder’’ tests of semantic processing. For example, of eight individuals (Nickels & Howard, 1994) who were impaired on synonym judgements (auditory or visual) four scored within normal limits on (PALPA spoken or written) word–picture matching. Hence, relatively good performance on PALPA word–picture matching should be interpreted with caution.

## Conclusions

This study has investigated the factors affecting spoken word–picture matching in aphasia. We have demonstrated that three variables (imageability, semantic similarity, and word association) have widespread effects, as demonstrated by significant effects for both the group and individuals within that group. It seems that for some people with aphasia, word–picture matching is performed more accurately when targets are of higher imageability, and are rated as less semantically similar to their semantic distractor, but have a higher degree of association. One variable (word frequency) was only significant at an individual (and not at a group) level, and this was not in the predicted direction—

targets of lower frequency were responded to more accurately. It was suggested that this may reflect a confound between frequency and semantic distinctiveness.

In sum, this study is one of very few investigating factors affecting comprehension in aphasia, and has raised important issues for further research.

## REFERENCES


Baayen, R. H., Piepenbrock, R., & Van Rijn (1993). *The CELEX lexical database* (CD-ROM). Linguistic Data Consortium, University of Pennsylvania, PA.

Best, W. (1995). A reverse length effect in dysphasic naming: When elephant is easier than ant. *Cortex, 31*, 637–652.

Bishop, D., & Byng, S. (1984). Assessing semantic comprehension: Methodological considerations and a new clinical test. *Cognitive Neuropsychology, 1*(3), 233–243.

Breedin, S. S., Saffran, E. M., & Coslett, H. B. (1994). Reversal of the concreteness effect in a patient with semantic dementia. *Cognitive Neuropsychology, 2*(6), 617–728.

Butterworth, B., Howard, D., & McLoughlin, P. (1984). The semantic deficit in aphasia: The relationship between semantic errors in auditory comprehension and picture naming. *Neuropsychologia, 22*(4), 409–426.

Caramazza, A. (1984). The logic of neuropsychological research and the problem of patient classification in aphasia. *Brain and Language, 21*, 9–20.

Cipolotti, L., & Warrington, E. K. (1995). Towards a unitary account of access dysphasia: A single case study. *Memory, 3*(3/4), 309–332.

Cole-Virtue, J., & Nickels, L. (2004). Spoken word to picture matching from PALPA: A critique and some new matched sets. *Aphasiology, 18*, 77–102.

Coltheart, M. (1980). The semantic error: Types and theories. In M. Coltheart, K. Patterson, & J. Marshall (Eds.), *Deep dyslexia*. London: Routledge & Kegan Paul.

Coltheart, M. (1981). The MRC psycholinguistic database. *Quarterly Journal of Experimental Psychology, 33*A, 497–505.

Coltheart, M., Patterson, K., & Marshall, J. C. (Eds.). (1980). *Deep dyslexia*. London: Routledge & Kegan Paul.

CSID (Computing and Information Systems Department (1996). *Edinburgh Associative Thesaurus*. Didcot, UK: Rutherford Appleton Laboratory UK.

Dunn, L. M., & Dunn, L. M. (1981). *Peabody Picture Vocabulary Test–Revised Manual*, Circle Pines, MN: American Guidance Service.

Forde, E., & Humphreys, G. W. (1995). Refractory semantics in global aphasia: On semantic organisation and the access–storage distinction in neuropsychology. *Memory, 3*(3/4), 265–307.

Forster, K. I. (1990). Lexical processing. In D.N. Osherson & H. Lasnik (Eds.), *Language: An invitation to cognitive science* (Vol 1, pp. 95–131). Cambridge, MA: MIT Press.

Franklin, S. (1989). Dissociations in auditory word comprehension: Evidence from nine fluent aphasic patients. *Aphasiology, 3*(3), 189–207.

Franklin, S., Howard, D., & Paterson, K. (1995). Abstract word anomia. *Cognitive Neuropsychology, 12*(5), 549–566.

Franklin, S., Turner, J., & Ellis, A. W. (1992). *The ADA Comprehension battery*. London: Action for Dysphasic Adults.

Franklin, S., Turner, J., Lambon Ralph, M. A., Morris, J., & Bailey, P. J. (1996). A distinctive case of word meaning deafness? *Cognitive Neuropsychology, 13*(8), 1139–1162.

Germani, M. J., & Pierce, R. S. (1995). Semantic attribute knowledge in adults with right and left hemisphere damage. *Aphasiology, 9*(1), 1–21.

Gilhooly, K. J., & Logie, R. H. (1980). Age-of-acquisition, imagery, concreteness, familiarity and ambiguity measures of 1944 words. *Behaviour Research Methods & Instruments, 12*, 395–427.

Goodglass, H., & Kaplan, E. (1972). *Assessment of aphasia and related disorders*. Philadelphia: Lea & Febiger.

Howard, D., & Franklin, S. (1988). *Missing the meaning*. London: MIT Press.

Kay, J., & Ellis, A. (1987). A cognitive neuropsychological case study of anomia: Implications for psychological models of word retrieval. *Brain, 110*, 613–629.

Kay, J., Lesser, R., & Coltheart, M. (1992). PALPA: *Psycholinguistic Assessments of Language Processing in Aphasia*. Hove, UK: Lawrence Erlbaum Associates Ltd.

Kay, J., Lesser, R., & Coltheart, M. (1996). Psycholinguistic assessments of language processing in aphasia (PALPA): An introduction. *Aphasiology, 10*, 159–179.

Kertesz, A. (1982). *The Western Aphasia Battery*. New York: Grune & Stratton Inc.

Lesser, R. (1981). *Linguistic Investigations of Aphasia*. London UK: Edward Arnold Publications.

Marshall, J., Pring, T., Chiat, S., & Robson, J. (2001). When ottoman is easier than chair: An inverse frequency effect in jargon aphasia. *Cortex, 37*, 33–53.

McRae, K., & Boisvert, S. (1998). Automatic semantic similarity priming. *Journal of Experimental Psychology: Learning, Memory and Cognition, 24*(3), 558–572.

Miceli, G., Amitrano, A., Capasso, R., & Caramazza, A. (1996). The treatment of anomia resulting from output lexical damage: Analysis of two cases. *Brain & Language, 52*, 150–174.

Morris, J. (1997). *Word deafness: A comparison of auditory and semantic treatments*. Unpublished doctoral dissertation, University of York, UK.

Morrison, C. M., Chappell, T. D., & Ellis, A. W. (1997). Age of acquisition norms for a large set of object names and their relation to adult estimates and other variables. *The Quarterly Journal of Experimental Psychology, 50*A(3), 528–559.

Morton, J. (1970). A functional model of memory. In D. A. Norman (Ed.), *Models of human memory*. New York: Academic Press.

Murphy, K. (1999). *The FIFO principle factors controlling retrieval speed in postcued partial report tasks*. Unpublished doctoral dissertation. Macquarie University, Sydney, Australia.

Nickels, L., & Howard, D. (1995). Aphasic naming: What matters? *Neuropsychologia, 33*(10), 1281–1303.

Nickels, L. (1997). Spoken word production and its breakdown in aphasia. Hove, UK: Psychology Press.

Neely, J. H. (1991). Semantic priming effects in visual word recognition: A selective review of current findings and theories. In D. Besner & G. W. Humphreys (Eds.) *Basic processes in reading: Visual word recognition*. Hillsdale, NJ: Lawrence Erlbaum Associates Inc.

Plaut, D. C., & Shallice, T. (1993). Deep dyslexia: A case study of connectionist neuropsychology. *Cognitive Neuropsychology, 10*(5), 377–500.

Schuell, H., Jenkins, J., & Landis, L. (1961). Relationship between auditory comprehension and word frequency in aphasia. *Journal of Speech and Hearing Research, 4*(1), 30–36.

# APPENDIX A

**Biographical details for participants with aphasia**

| *Subject* | *Age* | *Aetiology* | *Subject* | *Age* | *Aetiology* |
|---|---|---|---|---|---|
| AS | 83 | L.CVA | Ju | 67 | L.CVA |
| AE | 18 | L.CVA | JLB | 69 | L.CVA |
| AH | 70 | L.CVA | JT | 73 | L.CVA |
| BB | 57 | L.CVA | KE | 70 | L.CVA |
| BR | 38 | L.CVA | LAC | 65 | L.CVA |
| BD | 56 | L.CVA | LM | 75 | L.CVA |
| BT | 80 | L.CVA | LC | 69 | L.CVA |
| BM | 78 | L.CVA | LMT | 80 | L.CVA |
| BMcB | 78 | L.CVA | MC | 70 | L.CVA |
| CB | 71 | L.CVA | MiC | 56 | L.CVA |
| CO | 64 | L.CVA | MO | 78 | L.CVA |
| CP | / | L.CVA | MK | 72 | L.CVA |
| DJ | 31 | L.CVA | NC | 82 | L.CVA |
| DO | 55 | L.CVA | NW | / | L.CVA |
| EM | 78 | L.CVA | PD | / | L.CVA |
| FrS | 70 | L.CVA | PT | 50 | L.CVA |
| FS | 70 | L.CVA | RA | 60 | L.CVA |
| GV | 72 | L.CVA | RH | / | L.CVA |
| HC | / | L.CVA | RK | 86 | L.CVA |
| HE | 74 | L.CVA | SW | 24 | HI |
| HK | 59 | L.CVA | ShP | 65 | L.CVA |
| JO | 26 | HI | SG | 79 | L.CVA |
| JB | / | L.CVA | ST | 39 | L.CVA |
| JF | / | L.CVA | SP | / | L.CVA |
| JG | 65 | L.CVA | TB | / | L.CVA |
| J | 62 | L.CVA | VL | 55 | L.CVA |
| JuG | 41 | L.CVA | WB | 82 | L.CVA |

L.CVA: Left Cerebrovascular Accident; HI: Head injury.

# APPENDIX B

Intercorrelation matrix for psycholinguistic variables for stimuli from PALPA subtest 47

| | | *LF* | *Imag* | *Phon* | *Semsim* | *Vissim* | *T/CSD Freq diff* | *Assoc* |
|---|---|---|---|---|---|---|---|---|
| | Mean | 0.7 | 594.2 | 4.18 | 5.26 | 4.25 | 0.02 | 10.60 |
| | St Dev | 0.75 | 25.88 | 1.85 | 0.87 | 1.43 | 0.73 | 17.17 |
| | Range Min | −0.3 | 494 | 1 | 3.42 | 1.6 | −1.83 | 0 |
| | Range Max | 2.45 | 637 | 9 | 7 | 6.91 | 1.64 | 66 |
| LF | *r* | | 0.02 | −0.32 | 0.21 | 0.19 | 0.52 | 0.09 |
| | sig | | ns | 0.042 | ns | ns | 0.001 | ns |
| Imag | *r* | | | −0.01 | 0.20 | 0.09 | −0.10 | 0.04 |
| | sig | | | ns | ns | ns | ns | ns |
| Phon | *r* | | | | −0.36 | −0.32 | −0.15 | 0.10 |
| | sig | | | | 0.023 | 0.043 | ns | ns |
| Semsim | *r* | | | | | 0.66 | 0.14 | 0.04 |
| | sig | | | | | 0.000 | ns | ns |
| Vissim | *r* | | | | | | 0.12 | −0.25 |
| | sig | | | | | | ns | ns |
| T/CSD | | | | | | | | −0.1 |
| Freq diff | *r* | | | | | | | |
| | sig | | | | | | | ns |

LF: log frequency; Imag: rated imageability; Phon: number of phonemes; Semsim: semantic similarity rating between target and close semantic distractor; Vissim: visual similarity rating between target and close semantic distractor; T/CSD Freq diff: the difference between the target and close semantic distractor frequency; Assoc: word association; ns: non significant.

# APPENDIX C

## Control Group Errors

| | | *Close semantic distractor* | | | | | |
|---|---|---|---|---|---|---|---|
| *Target number* | *Target* | *non-SV* | *SV* | *Distant semantic distractor* | *Visual distractor* | *Unrelated distractor* | *No. errors per target* |
| Australian Control Group (*N* = 20*) | | | | | | | |
| 6 | belt | 0 | / | | 2 | | 2 |
| 10 | moon | 0 | / | 2 | | | 2 |
| 14 | stool | 0 | / | | 2 | | 2 |
| 25 | rake | / | 1 | | | | 1 |
| 30 | parachute | / | 2 | | 1 | | 3 |
| 38 | shoe | / | 1 | | | | 1 |
| 40 | stamp | | | | 1 | | 1 |
| No. distractor errors | | 0 | 4 | 2 | 6 | 0 | |
| Proportion of errors | | 0.00 | 0.33 | 0.17 | 0.50 | 0.00 | |
| British Control Group (*N* = 31**) | | | | | | | |
| 5 | axe | / | 1 | | 1 | | 2 |
| 7 | canoe | / | 1 | | | | 1 |
| 9 | television | / | 1 | | | | 1 |
| 10 | moon | 0 | / | 2 | | | 2 |
| 15 | syringe | 1 | / | | 1 | | 2 |
| 16 | crown | / | 2 | | | | 2 |
| 19 | lobster | / | 6 | | | | 6 |
| 20 | stirrup | 3 | / | | | | 3 |
| 28 | nail | / | 1 | | | | 1 |
| 39 | mug | / | 1 | | | | 1 |
| No. distractor errors | | 4 | 13 | 2 | 2 | 0 | |
| Proportion of errors | | 0.14 | 0.62 | 0.10 | 0.10 | 0.00 | |

Non-SV refers to close semantic distractors that are classified in PALPA as visually dissimilar to their respective targets; SV refers to close semantic distractors that are classified as visually similar to their respective targets.

* 9 subjects with errors

** 13 subjects with errors

# APPENDIX D

Correlations for Individual Aphasic Subject Performance for those subjects who showed correlations that were significant or approaching significance

| *Subject* | *Accuracy on subtest 47* ($n$ = 40) | | *Log frequency* | *Imageability* | *No. phonemes* | *Semantic similarity* | *Visual similarity* | *T/CSD frequency difference* | *Word association* |
|---|---|---|---|---|---|---|---|---|---|
| | | *N* | *40* | *35* | *40* | *40* | *40* | *40* | *35* |
| SW | 30 | *r* | −0.08 | 0.353 | −0.134 | −0.069 | 0.019 | 0.017 | −0.161 |
| | | *p* | 0.625 | **0.037** | 0.409 | 0.672 | 0.908 | 0.916 | 0.356 |
| PD | 29 | *r* | 0.172 | 0.362 | −0.217 | 0.035 | 0.013 | 0.157 | 0.056 |
| | | *p* | 0.289 | **0.033** | 0.179 | 0.831 | 0.937 | 0.333 | 0.751 |
| CB[1] | 38 | *r* | 0.096 | 0.674 | −0.103 | 0.181 | 0.082 | −0.165 | 0.087 |
| | | *p* | 0.556 | **0.000** | 0.525 | 0.263 | 0.614 | 0.31 | 0.619 |
| HE | 23 | *r* | 0.017 | 0.292 | 0.055 | −0.124 | −0.179 | −0.236 | 0.09 |
| | | *p* | 0.919 | 0.089 | 0.738 | 0.446 | 0.27 | 0.143 | 0.607 |
| RA | 34 | *r* | −0.024 | 0.4 | 0.002 | −0.224 | −0.258 | −0.078 | 0.154 |
| | | *p* | 0.883 | **0.017** | 0.991 | 0.165 | 0.108 | 0.632 | 0.376 |
| JG | 31 | *r* | 0.152 | −0.142 | −0.145 | −0.39 | −0.189 | −0.176 | 0.168 |
| | | *p* | 0.348 | 0.416 | 0.372 | **0.013** | 0.242 | 0.278 | 0.333 |
| JO | 35 | *r* | −0.177 | 0.067 | 0.326 | −0.458 | −0.21 | −0.085 | 0.039 |
| | | *p* | 0.273 | 0.701 | **0.04** | **0.003** | 0.194 | 0.601 | 0.826 |
| WB | 35 | *r* | 0.013 | −0.131 | 0.119 | −0.471 | −0.423 | −0.09 | 0.05 |
| | | *p* | 0.936 | 0.453 | 0.465 | **0.002** | **0.007** | 0.58 | 0.776 |
| HC[1,2] | 39 | *r* | 0.151 | | −0.422 | 0.313 | 0.101 | 0.005 | |
| | | *p* | 0.351 | | **0.007** | **0.049** | 0.537 | 0.976 | |
| LM | 20 | *r* | −0.273 | −0.01 | 0.342 | −0.25 | −0.081 | −0.033 | −0.192 |
| | | *p* | 0.089 | 0.955 | **0.031** | 0.119 | 0.62 | 0.842 | 0.27 |
| DO | 27 | *r* | −0.166 | 0.1 | 0.329 | −0.079 | −0.028 | −0.136 | 0.307 |
| | | *p* | 0.307 | 0.567 | **0.038** | 0.628 | 0.866 | 0.402 | 0.073 |
| BMcB | 36 | *r* | 0.004 | −0.032 | −0.424 | 0.101 | 0.234 | 0.048 | 0.635 |
| | | *p* | 0.98 | 0.856 | **0.006** | 0.534 | 0.146 | 0.77 | 0.083 |

(Continued overleaf)

## APPENDIX D

(Continued)

| *Subject* | *Accuracy on subtest 47 (n = 40)* | | *Log frequency* | *Imageability* | *No. phonemes* | *Semantic similarity* | *Visual similarity* | *T/CSD frequency difference* | *Word association* |
|---|---|---|---|---|---|---|---|---|---|
| | | *N* | *40* | *35* | *40* | *40* | *40* | *40* | *35* |
| SP[1] | 39 | *r* | 0.151 | −0.026 | −0.335 | 0.127 | −0.085 | 0.178 | 0.107 |
| | | *p* | 0.351 | 0.884 | **0.035** | 0.436 | 0.604 | 0.272 | 0.539 |
| AE | 33 | *r* | −0.036 | −0.254 | 0.332 | −0.244 | −0.341 | 0.074 | 0.191 |
| | | *p* | 0.827 | 0.141 | **0.036** | 0.13 | **0.031** | 0.65 | 0.272 |
| CO | 35 | *r* | 0.043 | 0.189 | −0.171 | −0.044 | −0.344 | −0.229 | 0.209 |
| | | *p* | 0.794 | 0.277 | 0.293 | 0.786 | **0.030** | 0.155 | 0.228 |
| FrS[1] | 38 | *r* | 0.086 | −0.104 | 0.147 | −0.22 | −0.335 | 0.177 | 0.038 |
| | | *p* | 0.599 | 0.551 | 0.364 | 0.172 | **0.035** | 0.274 | 0.829 |
| LMT | 33 | *r* | 0.334 | −0.234 | −0.1 | −0.007 | 0.076 | 0.036 | 0.097 |
| | | *p* | **0.035** | 0.176 | 0.54 | 0.965 | 0.64 | 0.825 | 0.581 |
| SG | 23 | *r* | −0.357 | −0.031 | 0.331 | −0.098 | −0.131 | −0.283 | 0.324 |
| | | *p* | **0.024** | 0.86 | **0.037** | 0.547 | 0.419 | 0.076 | 0.058 |
| HK | 26 | *r* | 0.186 | 0.043 | −0.13 | 0.024 | 0.014 | −0.267 | 0.304 |
| | | *p* | 0.25 | 0.804 | 0.423 | 0.883 | 0.933 | 0.096 | 0.076 |
| JuG | 18 | *r* | −0.123 | −0.095 | 0.106 | −0.265 | −0.141 | −0.172 | 0.257 |
| | | *p* | 0.448 | 0.588 | 0.516 | 0.098 | 0.386 | 0.29 | 0.135 |
| BB | 32 | *r* | 0.131 | 0.099 | −0.089 | 0.052 | −0.034 | −0.315 | 0.222 |
| | | *p* | 0.422 | 0.571 | 0.586 | 0.748 | 0.836 | **0.048** | 0.2 |
| EM | 34 | *r* | −0.117 | −0.16 | −0.036 | −0.115 | −0.229 | −0.329 | 0.167 |
| | | *p* | 0.471 | 0.358 | 0.824 | 0.479 | 0.155 | **0.038** | 0.339 |
| BR | 26 | *r* | −0.044 | 0.232 | −0.016 | −0.179 | −0.134 | −0.198 | 0.335 |
| | | *p* | 0.788 | 0.179 | 0.923 | 0.27 | 0.41 | 0.22 | **0.049** |

| | | | | | | | | | |
|---|---|---|---|---|---|---|---|---|---|
| AH | 31 | *r* | −0.098 | −0.041 | 0.215 | −0.302 | −0.19 | −0.074 | 0.124 |
| | | *p* | 0.546 | 0.815 | 0.182 | 0.058 | 0.24 | 0.649 | 0.478 |
| VL | 31 | *r* | −0.004 | 0.295 | 0.052 | 0.176 | 0.019 | −0.241 | 0.263 |
| | | *p* | 0.98 | 0.085 | 0.752 | 0.277 | 0.909 | 0.133 | 0.128 |
| JT | 36 | *r* | 0.288 | −0.114 | −0.105 | −0.126 | −0.103 | 0.099 | 0.038 |
| | | *p* | 0.072 | 0.516 | 0.52 | 0.44 | 0.526 | 0.543 | 0.829 |
| RH | 34 | *r* | 0.076 | −0.122 | −0.036 | −0.138 | −0.281 | −0.048 | 0.101 |
| | | *p* | 0.64 | 0.486 | 0.824 | 0.397 | 0.079 | 0.77 | 0.562 |
| MC | 33 | *r* | 0.303 | −0.038 | −0.244 | 0.248 | 0.2 | −0.096 | 0.103 |
| | | *p* | | 0.827 | 0.13 | 0.122 | 0.215 | 0.554 | 0.566 |
| MK | 24 | *r* | −0.121 | 0.208 | −0.201 | −0.311 | −0.175 | −0.295 | −0.092 |
| | | *p* | 0.457 | 0.231 | 0.214 | 0.051 | 0.279 | 0.065 | 0.601 |

[shaded] $p = < .10$

[boxed] $p = < .05$.

T/CSC Target/close semantic distractor

[1] These subjects performed within normal limits, we have included their data for the sake of completeness. However, when correlations are performed with such limited data, the robustness of any significant results must be questioned.

[2] This subject made only one error; imageability and word association values are not available for this item.

APHASIOLOGY, 2004, *18* (2), 181–183

# PALPA: What next?

Max Coltheart
*Macquarie University, Sydney, Australia*

What are we trying to do when we assess the language abilities of a person who has suffered a brain injury and whom we suspect may have aphasia; and why do we try to do it? Presumably the fundamental aim is to try to decide whether the brain injury has affected the person's abilities in some domain or domains of language. This aim is conceptually simple: We are notionally just comparing what the person's language was like prior to the brain injury with what it is like now, after the brain injury. If there are ways in which the language is worse now than it was then, it is reasonable to ascribe that difference to the effects of the brain injury.

This would not only be conceptually simple but also simple in practice if all brain-injured people suspected of having aphasia had had thorough language assessments prior to the brain injury. Since this will rarely if ever be so, it will rarely if ever be the case that one can compare the language abilities of a brain-injured person with what their language abilities were like prior to the injury. Given this, if we want to know whether the person's current language abilities have been impaired by the brain injury, the practical problem is: What can we compare these current abilities to?

This seems an absolutely fundamental question about the assessment of aphasia; but there's an even more fundamental question that needs to be considered first. It is: what do we mean by ''language abilities'' in the first place? No one thinks that language is a single ability: all agree that it is a set of abilities—but what are the components of this set? One can speak rather generally about syntactic, pragmatic, morphological, lexical, semantic, phonological, and orthographic abilities as comprising the set of abilities that constitute language. But cognitive-neuropsychological research has made it abundantly clear that none of these seven linguistic abilities is monolithic—all of them are composed of sub-abilities which are separably impairable by brain damage and so require to be separably assessable.

Progress cannot be made here unless we have some model of what the individual component abilities in each of these seven linguistic domains are. Any such model that is sufficiently explicit will immediately suggest ways in which one can exhaustively assess a person's abilities in each of these domains. That is the model-based assessment approach—the approach adopted in the construction of PALPA.

PALPA contains no material for the assessment of pragmatic disorders of language: It could not, because when it was being developed no model existed of what the individual processes are that go to make up the ability to use language in pragmatically appropriate ways. There still is no such model; perhaps in the future someone will develop a plausible

Address correspondence to: Max Coltheart, Macquarie Centre for Cognitive Science, Macquarie University, Sydney NSW 2109, Australia.


http://www.tandf.co.uk/journals/pp/02687038.html DOI:10.1080/02687030344000526

functional decomposition of the pragmatic language processing system, in which case it will be possible to add to PALPA a plausible set of tests of the components of pragmatic processing. PALPA tried to address the other six domains of language to at least some extent: The detail in which each domain was assessed was entirely driven by the level of detail of existing models of language processing in each domain. That is why the assessment of orthographic and phonological processing was so detailed, and the assessment of morphological and syntactic processing so sketchy, in the initial version of PALPA.

This is one force that will drive the future development of PALPA: It must wait upon further theoretical advances in the development of processing models of performance in the various language domains. But there is a second force at work here too, which the data of Kay and Terry (2004 this issue) illustrate via their documentation of the frequency of usage of the various PALPA subtests. Their literature search was unable to discover any publication reporting the use of PALPA Test 11: Repetition—Morphological endings, and only five uses of PALPA Test 34: Oral Reading—Morphological endings. This contrasts greatly with the 89 documented uses of PALPA Test 47: Spoken word—picture matching and the 84 documented uses of PALPA Test 47: Written word—picture matching. Why this neglect of morphology in comparison with semantics? It isn't because models of morphological processing in spoken word recognition or reading are rather unsophisticated (although they were and still are); it is surely because patients with impairments of semantic processing are much more common than patients with impairments of morphological processing. Given that, what should the developers of PALPA do if in the next few years there were rapid theoretical advances in our understanding of how morphological structure is processed in speech and print, and models of such detail were developed that fine-grained assessments of morphological processing deficits could be devised? Should such assessments be added to PALPA if the clinician will very rarely come across patients who have such deficits?

To some extent this issue has already arisen in the case of semantics. Since PALPA was published, cognitive neuropsychology has discovered a variety of intricate and highly specific semantic disorders selectively affecting specific semantic categories whilst sparing others. Does this mean that PALPA should include specific tests tapping comprehension of musical instruments, body parts, animals, vegetables and fruits, and man-made objects? Patients have been reported with specific comprehension impairments of such particular categories, but the overwhelming majority of patients with semantic impairment have a nonselective impairment affecting many or all semantic categories; thus, category-specific semantic tests would not be clinically useful. That is not to say that the existing PALPA tests of single-word comprehension do not require modification: the paper by Cole-Virtue and Nickels (2004 this issue) on the PALPA spoken and written picture–word matching tests indicates several ways in which the materials in these tests need to be improved.

So the future developers of PALPA must keep one eye on the lab and the other on the clinic.

As for the question with which I began this commentary: I think clinical aphasiology really needs to think much more deeply about the question of what norms are for. Suppose a clinician sees a client who has recently had a stroke, is now barely literate, and wants to take up a career in which adequate reading is essential. This client has come to the clinic because he wants treatment that will bring his reading up to the standard needed in his desired career. Exactly why does it matter here whether the client's reading was better before the stroke than it is now? Is this because it is believed that developmental dyslexia is more responsive to treatment than acquired dyslexia, so the prognosis for treatment depends on whether the stroke has anything to do with the client's poor reading? This can't be right, since we know nothing about the relative responsivity to treatment of acquired versus developmental disorders of language. If the basic idea of using normed tests of language performance is to try to estimate how different the brain-injured person's language is from what it was like prior to the injury—exactly why does the clinician want to know this? Why isn't it sufficient to obtain as detailed as possible a picture of what the client's language-processing system is like right now?

For Product Safety Concerns and Information please contact our EU representative GPSR@taylorandfrancis.com Taylor & Francis Verlag GmbH, Kaufingerstraße 24, 80331 München, Germany

**Batch number: 10726294**

Printed by Printforce, the Netherlands